D0984685

TRIAL

OF A

THOUSAND YEARS

HERBERT AND JANE DWIGHT WORKING GROUP
ON ISLAMISM AND THE INTERNATIONAL ORDER

Many of the writings associated with this
Working Group will be published by the Hoover Institution.
Materials published to date, or in production, are listed below.

ESSAYS

Saudi Arabia and the New Strategic Landscape
Joshua Teitelbaum

Islamism and the Future of the Christians of the Middle East
Habib C. Malik

Syria through Jihadist Eyes: A Perfect Enemy
Nibras Kazimi

The Ideological Struggle for Pakistan
Ziad Haider

BOOKS

Freedom or Terror: Europe Faces Jihad
Russell A. Berman

The Myth of the Great Satan: A New Look at America's Relations with Iran
Abbas Milani

Torn Country: Turkey between Secularism and Islamism
Zeyno Baran

Islamic Extremism and the War of Ideas: Lessons from Indonesia
John Hughes

Crosswinds: The Way of Saudi Arabia
Fouad Ajami

The End of Modern History in the Middle East
Bernard Lewis

The Wave: Man, God, and the Ballot Box in the Middle East
Reuel Marc Gerecht

Trial of a Thousand Years: World Order and Islamism
Charles Hill

Jihad in the Arabian Sea
Camille Pecastaing

HERBERT AND JANE DWIGHT WORKING GROUP ON ISLAMISM AND THE INTERNATIONAL ORDER

TRIAL
OF A
THOUSAND YEARS
World Order and *Islamism*

Charles Hill

HOOVER INSTITUTION PRESS
STANFORD UNIVERSITY | STANFORD, CALIFORNIA

www.hoover.org

Hoover Institution Press Publication No. 607

Hoover Institution at Leland Stanford Junior University, Stanford, California 94305-6010

First printing 2011
17 16 15 14 13 12 11   9 8 7 6 5 4 3 2 1

Manufactured in the United States of America

The paper used in this publication meets the minimum Requirements of the American National Standard for Information Sciences—Permanence of Paper for Printed Library Materials, ANSI/NISO Z39.48-1992. ⊗

Cataloging-in-Publication Data is available from the Library of Congress.

ISBN 978-0-8179-1324-3 (cloth. : alk. paper)
ISBN 978-0-8179-1326-7 (e-book)

To Fouad Ajami and John Raisian

HOOVER
INSTITUTION
STANFORD
UNIVERSITY

*The Hoover Institution gratefully acknowledges
the following individuals and foundations
for their significant support of the*

HERBERT AND JANE DWIGHT WORKING GROUP
ON ISLAMISM AND THE INTERNATIONAL ORDER:

Herbert and Jane Dwight
Stephen Bechtel Foundation
Lynde and Harry Bradley Foundation
Mr. and Mrs. Clayton W. Frye Jr.
Lakeside Foundation

CONTENTS

FOREWORD

FOR DECADES, THE THEMES of the Hoover Institution have revolved around the broad concerns of political, economic, and individual freedom. The cold war that engaged and challenged our nation during the twentieth century guided a good deal of Hoover's work, including its archival accumulation and research studies. The steady output of work on the communist world offers durable testimonies to that time and struggle. But there is no repose from history's exertions, and no sooner had communism left the stage of history than a huge challenge arose in the broad lands of the Islamic world. A brief respite and a meandering road led from the fall of the Berlin Wall on 11/9 in 1989 to 9/11. Hoover's newly launched project, the Herbert and Jane Dwight Working Group on Islamism and the International Order, is our contribution to a deeper understanding of the struggle in the Islamic world between order and its nemesis, between Muslims keen to protect the rule of reason and the gains of modernity and those determined to deny the Islamic world its place in the modern international order of states. The United States is deeply engaged, and dangerously exposed, in the Islamic world, and we see our working group as part and parcel of the ongoing confrontation with the radical Islamists who have declared war on the states in their midst, on American power and interests, and on the very order of the international state system.

The Islamists are doubtless a minority in the world of Islam. But they are a determined breed. Their world is the Islamic emirate, led by self-styled "emirs and mujahedeen in the path of God" and legitimized by the pursuit of the caliphate that collapsed with the end of the Ottoman Empire in 1924. These masters of terror and their foot soldiers have made it increasingly difficult to integrate the world of Islam into modernity. In the best of worlds, the entry of Muslims into modern culture and economics would have presented difficulties of no small consequence: the strictures on women, the legacy of humiliation and self-pity, the outdated educational systems, and an explosive demography that is forever at war with social and economic gains. But the borders these warriors of the faith have erected between Islam and "the other" are particularly forbidding. The lands of Islam were the lands of a crossroads civilization, trading routes, and mixed populations. The Islamists have waged war—and a brutally effective one, it has to be conceded—against that civilizational inheritance. The leap into the modern world economy as attained by China and India in recent years will be virtually impossible in a culture that feeds off belligerent self-pity and endlessly calls for wars of faith.

The war of ideas with radical Islamism is the central pillar of this Hoover endeavor. The strategic context of this clash is the landscape of that Greater Middle East. We face three layers of danger in the heartland of the Islamic world: states that have succumbed to the sway of terrorists in which state authority no longer exists (Afghanistan, Somalia, and Yemen), dictatorial regimes that suppress their people at home and pursue deadly weapons of mass destruction and adventurism abroad (Iraq under Saddam Hussein, the Iranian theocracy), and "enabler" regimes, such as the ones in Egypt and Saudi Arabia, which export their own problems with radical Islamism to other parts of the Islamic world and beyond. In this context, the task of reversing Islamist radicalism and of reforming and strengthening the state across the entire Muslim world—the Middle East and Africa, as well as South, Southeast, and Central Asia—is the greatest strategic challenge of the twenty-first century. The essential starting point is detailed knowledge of our enemy.

Thus, the working group will draw on the intellectual resources of the Hoover Institution and Stanford University and on an array of scholars and practitioners from elsewhere in the United States, the Middle East, and the broader world of Islam. The scholarship on contemporary Islam can now be read with discernment. A good deal of it, produced in the immediate aftermath of 9/11, was not particularly deep and did not stand the test of time and events. We, however, are in the favorable position of a "second generation" assessment of that Islamic material. Our scholars and experts can report in a detailed, authoritative way on Islam within the Arabian Peninsula, on trends within Egyptian Islam, and on the struggle between the Kemalist secular tradition in Turkey and the new Islamists, particularly the fight for the loyalty of European Islam between those who accept the canon, and the discipline, of modernism and those who don't.

Arabs and Muslims need not be believers in American exceptionalism, but our hope is to engage them in this contest of ideas. We will not necessarily aim at producing primary scholarship, but such scholarship may materialize in that our participants are researchers who know their subjects intimately. We see our critical output as essays accessible to a broader audience, primers about matters that require explication, op-eds, writings that will become part of the public debate, and short, engaging books that can illuminate the choices and the struggles in modern Islam.

We see this endeavor as a faithful reflection of the values that animate a decent, moderate society. We know the travails of modern Islam, and this working group will be unsparing in depicting them. But we also know that the battle for modern Islam is not yet lost, that there are brave men and women fighting to retrieve their faith from the extremists. Some of our participants will themselves be intellectuals and public figures who have stood up to the pressure. The working group will be unapologetic about America's role in the Muslim world. A power that laid to waste religious tyranny in Afghanistan and despotism in Iraq, that came to the rescue of the Muslims in the Balkans when they appeared all but doomed, has given much to those burdened populations. We haven't always understood Islam and Muslims—hence this inquiry. But it is a given of the working group that the pursuit of modernity and human welfare, and of the rule of law and reason, in Islamic lands is the common ground between America and contemporary Islam.

Two quotations provide the bookends of a great debate about the place of the state in the modern world order, and frame this book of startling originality by Charles Hill. The first is from Georg Wilhelm Friedrich Hegel, who memorably wrote, "It is the way of God with the world that the state exists." The second is closer to us in time, coming from the teachings of the Egyptian Sayyid Qutb, a signal figure in the world of political Islam who was executed by the secular regime in his homeland in 1966: "A Muslim has no nationality except his religious beliefs." We know of course that God has not made the state; the Treaty of Westphalia did so in 1648, decreeing that religion be banished from the quarrels of states. Sayyid Qutb erred, too. The Muslim states may have been feeble and ill-at-ease in the world of nations, but they have been knocking at the gates of the modern order of states, pining for its protections and insignia along with the self-respect that comes with statehood.

In this remarkable book—beguiling in its mastery of history, effortless in its wanderings through time and geography— Charles Hill tackles a subject that has been begging to be written: the war of Islamism against the nation-state system, the refusal of the ideologues of pan-Islam to accept the boundaries and the limitations of the order of states. From a scholar and diplomatic practitioner of incomparable skills and learning comes this unique inquiry into the challenge that the Islamists pose for our contemporary order of nations. A historian and a student of strategy at home in the classics and the corridors of power alike, Hill places the Islamists in their proper historical place. They are but the latest challenge, he tells us, to the restrictions that states had placed on themselves since the state system was born in 1648. There have been other assaults on the house of nations that states built and agreed to inhabit. The French Revolution warred against the order of its time. In their zeal, the French revolutionaries insisted that their "revolution-ary happiness" belonged to all the nations around them. There was France as a state and France as a "sect," Edmund Burke famously wrote of that radical new challenge. The sect tram-pled upon national boundaries; it came to Europe, as Burke so aptly put it, as both panacea and plague. It would take a quarter-century before this revolution was made to accept the integrity of the system of states. Imperial Japan and Nazi Germany hurled themselves against the restrictions and workings of their world. And, of course, there was communism's taxing and long chal-lenge. Lesser contenders have turned up now and then only to be turned back. (Perhaps God does look after the state, after all.) For the Islamists, this diplomatic order, constructed by unbeliev-ers, accepted by regimes of apostates in the Islamic world, is no order of theirs; its scruples and restrictions are not theirs.

There once were mighty Islamic states, imperial orders of reach and power; the Ottomans, the Mughals, the Persians were powers of consequence in the sixteenth century. The European world overwhelmed them. The Ottoman Turks came closest to victory, contesting for primacy in the Eastern Medi-terranean and beyond. Sixteenth-century European prophecies forecast the Ottomans upending the peace of Europe, conquer-ing Rome itself. But Ottoman power faltered, the Turks fell behind, their empire became a plaything of outsiders, "the sick man of Europe." The Islamists know that history and the fall of the caliphate, its utter and solitary end in 1924. Still, there plays on memory that brief time of Islam's triumph in its first two centuries. All this is of the past, and this order of states, as Hill writes, has become "every civilization's *other* civilization, addressing a natural need, much as diverse species depend on a common ecosystem." To this, the Islamists are strangers, and determined enemies. They war against the world order and against the Pax Americana that guards its peace. There is intellectual vigilance in this book, but poise as well. Hill cherishes this order, but knows it is always in need of repair, that it always must be nourished and defended. Those jihadists at war with the contemporary order receive here the searching scrutiny they deserve.

Sayyid Qutb's followers are no small challenge to the practices and values of our universal civilization—to that common ecosystem. In that zone between the failures of the Muslim states and the illusions and abdications of the democracies, that "sect" thrives and assaults the order of states. In Hill's reflections, the terms of engagement between the order and its enemies are laid out with unflinching rigor and clarity, in luminous prose.

FOUAD AJAMI

Senior Fellow, Hoover Institution
Cochairman, Herbert and Jane Dwight Working Group
on Islamism and the International Order

TRIAL

OF A

THOUSAND YEARS

From *Studies at Delhi*, 1876:

II.—Badminton

Hardly a shot from the gate we stormed,
    Under the Moree battlement's shade;
Close to the glacis our game was formed,
    There had the fight been, and there we played.

Lightly the demoiselles tittered and leapt,
    Merrily capered the players all;
North, was the garden where Nicholson slept,
    South, was the sweep of a battered wall.

Near me a Musalmán, civil and mild,
    Watched as the shuttlecocks rose and fell;
And he said, as he counted his beads and smiled,
    'God smite their souls to the depths of hell.'

SIR ALFRED COMYNS LYALL

PROLOGUE

ON A SHIP TO OMAN

Twenty years ago, a ship that was calling at some of the hell-hole ports on the Indian Ocean and Arabian Sea put in for water at Salalah, Oman. It was then a dusty, sun-stroked town with no sights to see. We walked aimlessly down an un-busy main street. A boy ran out. "Do you want to see Job's tomb?" We did, surprised to learn that this was the resting place of the Biblical sufferer. On a hill beyond the town, Jabal Qara, we were led to a small mosque and shown a green-silk, gold-embroidered shroud-draped slab, more than twice the length of a man. (They were big then, we were told.) It was one of those strangely enchanted places where you instinctively feel, "Yes—this really is what they claim it is: the Tomb of Job."

Several years later when teaching the Book of Job in the Hebrew Bible as part of Yale's Directed Studies (i.e., great books) course, I read William Safire's interpretation of the Hebrew Bible's Job as "the first dissident," and then looked up Job in the Quran. The Islamic Job had been terribly afflicted by God; later God was merciful and Job's miseries ended. God is great, omnipotent; that's all you need to know. The reading in what we might dare call the Judeo-Christian tradition was different. Job does not have "the patience of Job." He speaks out, to contest God's apparently pointless exercise of power. A political interaction

3

has begun between man and Maker, and both may learn from the encounter.

PHILOLOGISTS CONCLUDE that the Book of Job in the Hebrew Bible does not come out of the Jewish tradition, but is an insertion from another, more ancient source, perhaps Sumerian, or the land of "Uz" where Job was said to dwell, wherever that was.

The story of Job is featured in Oswald Spengler's analysis of "Magian," i.e., pre-Islamic, culture in Spengler's enigmatically powerful *Untergang des Abendlandes* (*The Decline of the West*). The Job story, Spengler says, is the epitome of the Magian idea of Grace which "forms a contrast of the deepest intensity with the Faustian (Spengler's term for the West) idea of Contrition." Contrition pre-supposes the will of an ego, but Grace knows of no such thing. The idea of Grace excludes every individual will and every cause but the One, so that it is sinful even to question why man suffers. It is not Job but his friends who look for a sin as the cause of his troubles or presume that they are God's way of testing the sufferer's faith. In the Magian realm, Spengler says, they do not grapple with the ultimate meaning of life.

To explain the larger context, Spengler borrowed a term from mineralogy: "pseudomorphosis." That is when embedded crystals are geologically blocked from taking their natural form. In the human case, when an alien power lies on a culture so that it cannot get its breath, cannot develop its self-consciousness, this causes the culture—the Magian—to "hate the distant power with a hate that grows to be monstrous."

So, Spengler says, from about 300 B.C. on, a great awakening of peoples took place between the desert of Sinai and the mountains of Zagros, a new relationship of man to God. But just at this moment came Alexander the Great's Macedonians, who "laid down a thin sheet of Classical (i.e., Western) civilization stretching as far as Turkestan and India." Thus the characteristically Magian elements were squeezed into alien forms and distorted by the logic of a different civilization.

What did pseudomorphosis do to this new Magian relationship of man to God? The classical religion was local and separated into cults, with each divinity bounded in its own geographic place. The Magian religion was in sharp contrast: a community of believers whose creed knew no earthly frontier—but which was not allowed its natural, unbounded space.

Magian culture, Spengler says, finally took up its swift, passionate tempo with the rise of Islam, "a religion *only formally new*; this is what explains its fabulously swift successes." "This alone," he writes, "is sufficient to explain the intense vehemence with which the Arabian Culture, when released at length from artistic as from other fetters, flung itself upon all the lands that had inwardly belonged to it for centuries past. It is the sign of a soul that feels itself in a hurry, that notes in fear the first symptoms of old age before it has had youth. This emancipation of Magian mankind is without parallel. In these few years (634 to 732) was compressed the whole sum of saved-up passions, postponed hopes, reserved deeds, that in the slow

maturing of other cultures suffice to fill the history of centuries." Job, who lived and suffered in the far antiquity of the
pre-Islamic Magian culture, could now find his natural form
among the Muslim believers as, in Arabic, Ayoub.

On the Train to the Army-Navy Game

In 1970, with the United States at a low point in the cold war
contest with the Soviet Union, the U.S. Navy's Chief of Naval
Operations, Admiral Elmo R. Zumwalt, invited Henry Kissinger,
the dominant figure in American foreign policy, to ride the
Navy's special train to Philadelphia for the Army-Navy game.
According to Zumwalt, on board the train Kissinger spoke about
America's decline and his task of persuading the Russians to give
us the best deal we could get in our weakening condition. The
American people lack stamina, Kissinger said, while the Soviets
are "Sparta to our Athens"; in other words, we were fated to collapse. The newspapers had the story at once. It was "Spenglerian,"
referring to Spengler's famous 1918 opus *The Decline of the West*,
a subject of Kissinger's college thesis on "The Meaning of
History." The story spread quickly. Kissinger sharply denied
it, saying Zumwalt deserved "the Nobel Prize for Fiction."

Spengler's declinism has affected the Arab-Islamic world.
The Syrian philosopher Sadiq Jalal Al-Azm noted that sophisticated Islamist thinkers and theoreticians draw from "a con-
stellation of ideas captured in the title of a European classic,
Spengler's *Decline of the West*, the implication that if the West
is declining then the Arab world must be rising" and on the

verge of retrieving its usurped role of world-historical leadership. Only Islam could restore Arab power to the height from
which it could not fall because the sacred would eternally
endure.

As Sadiq Al-Azm put it,

> this means that such values as liberalism,
> secularism, democracy, human rights, religious
> toleration, freedom of expression, etc. are to be
> regarded as the West's deepest values, from
> which the contemporary Muslim World is permanently
> excluded on account of its most deeply cherished
> values—theocracy, theonomy, scripturalism,
> literalism, fundamentalism, communalism,
> totalitarianism, sexism, absolutism, and
> dogmatism . . .

This would appear to be a fundamental obstacle to the
achievement of any kind of shared system for world order.

CHAPTER ONE

Two World Orders

W ORLD ORDER HAS BEEN a matter for the modern age, taken up seriously in the time and context of the seventeenth-century intersection of the European and Islamic crosscurrents. Before this, empires might believe themselves cosmic in scale and divine in significance while actually ruling over only a portion of the globe, unaware of the whole.

In 1887, in a low brick room at Tel al-Amarna, a peasant woman stumbled upon an archive of documents relating to the foreign affairs of Akhenaten (Amenhotep IV), revealing inten-sive diplomatic contacts among the great powers of that time. A mixed language that scholars called "Amarnaic" served as an agreed diplomatic means of communication among Egypt, Babylonia, the Hittites, the Canaanites, Mittani (Syria), and other states, the torso of an international system for the Late Bronze Age, the first of its kind. The system was made up of state-like polities of different cultures and languages, unequal in power yet accepting common practices, operating through diplomacy, alliances and treaties, trading for mutual advantage, keeping records and establishing precedents, and maintaining their independence while aiming to avoid war within an understood framework.

Pre-modern China produced its own versions. The Spring and Autumn Period, 770–476 B.C., displayed a political-economic-military system among the several Han kingdoms of north-central China. Much later, with the rise of dynasties whose reach extended well beyond China proper—the T'ang, Sung, Yuan, Ming, and Ch'ing—a tribute system, with the Imperial Court as the world center, regulated international relations.

As the Roman Empire slowly succumbed to waves of barbarian assault, Christianity presented itself as a universalist system, shaping itself from the founding of Constantinople in 330 A.D. in the East to the coronation of Otto I as Holy Roman Emperor in 962 in the West as Christendom. Christianity defined its project as building a world order to overcome paganism. Thus the rise of Islam came as a profound shock.

The Islamic world produced its own idea of an international system, the caliphate. No earlier institution undergirded it. With the death of the Prophet in 632 A.D., follow-on leadership was a practical necessity. No one at the beginning of the seventh century, Arab or not, could have anticipated the vast extent, the immense wealth and power, which would be under the control of the successor of the Prophet when he ruled at Damascus or Baghdad.

CHRISTENDOM AND CALIPHATE

So in the early Middle Ages two substantive world systems, Christendom and Islam, each focused on and guided by a divine conviction, faced each other largely ignorant and entirely unappreciative of one another's ideals. As the historian of late antiquity Peter Brown put it, "For the first time, half the known world took on an alien face." When Pope Innocent III declared that the Lord had entrusted to Peter not only the Universal Church, but the government of the whole world, the Holy Roman Empire took as its aim a world-state in which the emperor would be the universal sovereign. Similarly, Islam, a universal faith, expected the submission of all men and women, who must either accept the message of the Prophet or pay tribute as subject peoples, all under the Prophet's successor, the caliphate.

The two world-systems were fundamentally different. The Holy Roman Empire was a conscious revival of the pre-Christian Roman Empire transposed into a Christian dominium linking the City of God to the City of Man; Charlemagne was a reader of St. Augustine's magnum opus. But, critically important, side-by-side with the emperor was the pope, who possessed spiritual authorities denied to the emperor. Dante would elaborate on this in his *De Monarchia*, one of the most consequential works of political theory in history. Dante made the separation of church and state a God-decreed imperative—his key argument being that in order for Christ to die for men's sins, He had to be legally condemned by a governing authority for all the world; that was the Roman Empire. Thus a legitimate non-religious ruler was an indispensible part of God's plan, meant to rule apart from and not under God's church. The pope would be the vicar of God on earth, representing the City of God and guiding men's souls thither; the emperor would maintain order over men's bodies so that the greater work of God might proceed with as little disruption as possible in what was, after all, a fallen world. Throughout the centuries during which the Holy Roman Empire was a force in Europe, the distinction between spiritual and temporal authority was never lost sight of.

The caliphate emerged wholly otherwise. The theory of the office was not invented until after the Arab empire had become an accomplished reality; it was extracted from the Hadith, the collected sayings of the Prophet and his companions, oral traditions which eventually became a second source of authority with the Quran. The practical theory located there implied that all earthly authority is by divine appointment. Whether the ruler is just or unjust, the duty of subjects is to obey, because responsibility rests with God. The Hadith declared, "When God wishes good for a people, He sets over them the forbearing and wise, and places their goods in the hands of generous rulers; but when God wishes evil for a people, He sets over them the witless and base and extracts their goods to avaricious rulers." The power of the caliph was limited in only one respect: he, like every Muslim, must submit to *sharia*, the law grounded in the will of God—so there was no room for the distinction that arose in Christendom between canon law and the law of the state.

DUALITY OR UNITY?

"There are two kinds of people," the old saying goes, "those who say there are two kinds of people and those who don't." Beneath this sardonic comment lies a profound difference between cultures or civilizations. F. Scott Fitzgerald, presuming that he was speaking for the entire human condition, declared that "the ability to hold two contradictory ideas in the mind at the same time and still function is a test of civilization."

Not so for Islamists. The Catholic intellectual Father Richard John Neuhaus wrote that, in jihadi eyes, "The most fundamental error of Western liberalism is the distinction, even division, of sacred and profane," resulting in what the influential Egyptian Islamist Sayyid Qutb termed "hideous schizophrenia." Thus Islamists vehemently reject dualities while the West is foundationally defined by them. Judaic thought was marked by binary classifications; the philosophers of classical Athens and the theologians of Christian Rome explained duality as humanity's essential nature. Plato's work proceeds by way of Socratic dialogue. Aristotle's *Politics* explains the achievement of civilization through the dualities of theory and practice, ends and means, and culminates in what the philosopher terms as Dorian and Phrygian "modes": male and female principles which need to be kept in balance.

Plato and Aristotle themselves became a duo, as depicted in Raphael's monumental painting, "The School of Athens," in which the two walk side by side, Plato pointing up toward the metaphysical "forms" as Aristotle gestures downward

toward the things of this world, all of which require intellectual investigation.

Augustine institutes dualities all through his massive *City of
God* with its earthly counterpart to the City of Man: body and
soul, fate and free will, the two kinds of morality—individual
and societal, reason and revelation, and so on.

Thomas Aquinas would synthesize Plato and Aristotle, and
Augustine as well, in his comprehensive *Summa Theologicae*: this
world and the next were dualistic but linked. The study of earthly
reality will reveal reflections of God's reality. Thomas opened the
way for science to seek progress in a way compatible, not adversarial, to God's realm. Western civilization would lead the world,
or much of it, into modernity, as the Muslim world, once the
leader, would subside in proportion to its antagonism toward the
dual and insistence on the uniate.

Thus has Islam defined itself by its purist monotheism and
relentless rejection of duality, triplicity, pluralism, and multifariousness. Yet this uniate focus did not impair the remarkable
record of Muslim flourishing in virtually all of the arts and sciences during the early centuries of the faith's rise to world
power. As Fernand Braudel noted, "Paradoxical as it may seem,
Islamic civilization as a whole, between 813 and 1198 (i.e.,
from the Caliphate of al-Mamun to the death of Averroes) was
both one and many, universal and regionally diverse." Islamic
philosophy began to integrate the thought of Aristotle. The
results were astonishing achievements in science, mathematics,
astronomy, chemistry, optics, and recognition of the circulation of the blood—three centuries before William Harvey demonstrated it at Oxford.

What then happened to cause the decline from which Islamic culture still has not recovered? Explanations vary. Was it the loss of territorial control to Christian, Mongol, and Turkish forces? Or the increasing decadence among the elite akin to that which corrupted Rome as depicted by Tacitus? Often cited were "the powerful, desperate blows to free thought" in the eleventh century by one of the most influential figures in all intellectual history, Abu Hamid Muhammed al-Ghazali (1058–1111). He was a thinker of the *ulema* known as the Proof of Islam (*hujja al-islam*) whose work supposedly refuted Aristotelian reason to the extent of leading Muslim minds to turn away from scientific studies. (Yet, so brilliantly did al-Ghazali describe Aristotelianism that European scholars began to adopt his interpretation of the philosopher's thought). Algazel, as he was known in the West, was depicted as a kind of anti-Aquinas, determined not to reconcile reason and revelation, but to crown revelation over all, and to return the faith to its earliest, simplest dogmatic precepts. Whether al-Ghazali was a cause or a symptom, or neither, of the downward turn, in the twelfth century Muslim civilization suddenly stalled.

Yet the decline of the Arab-Islamic empire was also the time when systematic study of the caliphate's role was undertaken. Evidence in the Hadith that the caliph should be a member of the Prophet's tribe, the Quraysh, was joined by scholars' rulings that the office was elective—which fit the reality that almost every caliph had nominated his successor. To be eligible for election, one must both be a Qurayshi and possess the qualities needed to defend and extend the faith.

The record indicates that Islam's unswerving devotion to monotheism did not, during its early centuries, block great achievements in arts and sciences dependent on free thought. But once turned in on itself, the Muslim mind closed for centuries.

Christian fear and hatred of Islam during the Middle Ages was nourished by the tall tales of pilgrims and the fiery words of crusading preachers. Some Europeans assumed Muslims worshipped Muhammad as a god, but mainly he was thought a heretic. The Western attitude toward the Prophet was captured by Dante in *Inferno* XXVIII when the poet and Virgil are touring the Eighth Circle of Hell, where the Sowers of Schism perpetually circled, each wounded by a demon who, as the wound healed, maimed the heretic again:

> See now how maimed Mohammad is! And he
> who walks and weeps before me is Ali,
> whose face is opened wide from chin to forelock.
> And all the others here whom you can see
> were, when alive, the sowers of dissension
> and scandal, and for this they now are split.

Dante is aware of Ali, the Prophet's cousin and son-in-law, as the loser in the conflict over the caliphate. Dante may be saying here that if Mohammad is a heretic to Christianity, Ali is a heretic to "Mohammadism."

In 1219, Francis of Assisi and a few fellow friars went to the Islamic world, seeking to call on the Sultan in Egypt and to live quietly among Muslims as "lesser brothers." With the Fifth

Crusade under way, it was a remarkable gesture, and perhaps a dangerous one. Francis found Muslims to be filled with God's spirit and admired their five daily prayers and reverence for the Quran. The Franciscans apparently made no lasting impact on their hosts; influence may have gone the other way. Some claim Francis brought back to Christendom the idea of the rosary based on Muslim prayer beads, or that the thrice-daily Angelus soon to be adopted in Europe was a version of Muslim prayer. G. K. Chesterton, in his biography of St. Francis, calls it a moment when the course of the world might have been changed, but wasn't. More likely, Francis's expedition simply showed the limitations of good will humbly expressed.

From the Muslim side, contrary to widespread modern belief, Muslim and non-Muslim, the Crusades were not regarded at the time as the monumentally alienating episode they are assumed to be today. Far more important and alarming for Islam were the disastrous Mongol invasions, with the horde of Hulagu capturing Baghdad in 1258 and putting the Abbasid caliph to death.

"The Turk" and "Oriental Despotism"

Of great concern to the Muslim and Christian worlds alike was the sudden resurgence and re-expansion of Islam after 1300 as the Turks, Islamicized steppe-warriors, plunged into Muslim, Christian, and Hindu lands alike. In Anatolia—Asia Minor— the Turkish leader Osman founded a state which became the core of the future Ottoman Empire. By the end of the century they were masters of the European Balkans. The caliphate was claimed by Osman's grandson Murad I (1326–1389), who forced Byzantium to pay tribute and led his army to victory on the famous Field of the Blackbirds in 1389, bringing Serbia under Turkish rule.

These newly powerful Turks, wrote the historian Steven Runciman, "were barbarous and destructive. They had become Muslims and acquired a thin veneer of Persian culture, but that was all." Runciman's classic work on the fall of Constantinople to the Turks opens with a vivid scene:

> On Christmas Day in the year 1400 King Henry IV of England gave a banquet in his palace of Eltham. His purpose was not only to celebrate the holy festival. He wished also to do honour to a distinguished guest. This was Manuel II Palaeologus, Emperor of the Greeks, as most Westerners called him, though some remembered that he was the true Emperor of the Romans. He had travelled through Italy and had paused at Paris, where King Charles VI of France had redecorated a wing of the Louvre to house him and where the professors at the Sorbonne had been delighted to meet a monarch who could argue with them with as much learning and subtlety as they themselves commanded. In England everyone was impressed by the dignity of his demeanor and by the spotless white robes that he and his courtiers wore. But, for all his high titles, his hosts were moved to pity for him; for he had come as a beggar, in a desperate search for help against the infidel who encompassed his empire. To the lawyer Adam of Usk, who was working at King Henry's court, it was tragic to see him there. "I reflected," Adam wrote, "how grievous it was that this great Christian prince should be driven by the Saracens from the furthest East to these furthest

Western islands to seek aid against them . . . O God," he added, "what dost thou now, ancient glory of Rome?"

The end came in 1453 after a hopeless but heroic defense of seven weeks. Within a few years following, the Ottoman Turks had destroyed the concept of a Roman-Christian-Greek empire and had established the reality of Ottoman dominance across Asia Minor and the entire eastern Mediterranean. The news that Constantinople had fallen to the Turks was received in the West with horror and foreboding. The victorious Sultan Mehmed II was cited as declaring, "Our empire is the home of Islam; from father to son the lamp of our empire is kept burning with oil from the hearts of the infidels."

Perhaps Byzantium had been fated to fall because history's proper direction had been violated. Since the fall of Troy and Aeneas's mission to found Rome, the course of empire was supposed to move from east to west; the decision to shift Christianity's center of power to Constantinople had gone against the *translatio imperii et studii*, tempting fate. Now a Turkish advance on Rome was expected.

So from the later fourteenth century to the beginning of the twentieth, Europeans tended to identify Islam with the Ottoman Empire. Hostility to "The Turk" was almost an article of faith. In 1480 a Dominican Friar sent a tract to Pope Sixtus IV and the major monarchs of Christian Europe proposing that the Prophet Muhammad was the Anti-Christ. While most Christian prophecies foretold the ultimate doom of the Turks, from the reign of Sultan Murad II in 1421 the Ottomans had been ever-victorious: they crushed the Persians in 1514 and proceeded to overrun

Kurdistan in 1515, Syria and Palestine in 1516, and Egypt in 1517. When Selim I captured Cairo, the last tattered claim of the Abbasids to the caliphate ended; none were left to question the full rights of the Ottomans to the title. With the caliphate entirely in Turkish hands there were no more scholarly assertions that the office must be held by a member of the Prophet's lineage, the Quraysh. The caliphate had been taken by the sword and justified as the will of Allah. The Ottoman advance had been stopped at Belgrade; but at Otranto, on the tip of Italy's heel, the Turks had established a beachhead for an assault on Rome. The Order of the World was at stake.

The great aura surrounding the Ottoman court in its Topkapi Palace, where construction began in 1459, only intensified with the perception of visitors that its nearest analogue, perhaps its model, was to be found in Plato's *Republic*. The early twentieth-century American scholar Albert Lybyer wrote, "Perhaps no more daring experiment has been tried on a large scale on the face of the earth than that embodied in the Ottoman Ruling Institution . . . as near to [Plato's] plan as it is possible to come in a workable scheme."

> The Ottoman system deliberately took slaves and made them ministers of state; it took boys from the sheep-run and made them courtiers and the husbands of princesses; it took young men whose ancestors had borne the Christian name for centuries, and made them rulers in the greatest of Mohammedan states, and soldiers and generals in invincible armies whose chief joy was to beat down the Cross and elevate the Crescent.
> . . . Grandly disregarding the fabric of fundamental customs which is called "human nature," and those religious and social

prejudices which are thought to be almost as deep as life itself, the Ottoman system took children from parents, discouraged family cares among its members through their most active years, allowed them no certain hold on property, gave them no definite promise that their sons and daughters would profit by their success and sacrifice, raised and lowered them with no regard for ancestry or previous distinction, taught them a strange law, ethics, and religion, and ever kept them conscious of a sword raised above their heads which might put an end at any moment to a brilliant career along a matchless path of human glory.

The members of this system were, in a generous way, as long as they lived, at once slaves, proselytes, students, soldiers, nobles, courtiers, and officers of government. To be understood fully, the institution should be considered from each of these points of view. The aspects which were of central and controlling importance, however, were those of war and government; the others were preparatory or accessory.

Lybyer, a pioneering scholar of the Ottoman Empire, recently has been disparaged as an "Orientalist" and purveyor of "a distorted schematization." Perhaps, but later scholars of the Grand Porte, the Seraglio, and the Palace School also observed that the curriculum, career patterns, and rigorously imposed system seemed prima facie evidence of Plato's influence, and the idea of an exotic, despotic, Eastern utopia took hold.

The Ottoman Empire as a version of Plato's Republic would not be the only time a Middle Eastern regime appeared to model itself on a centralizing Western ideology, as we will see later with the Islamic Republic of Iran.

In the sixteenth century the image of "The Red Apple" arose, symbolizing world dominion. The Abbot of Otranto promulgated an apocalyptic vision: the Turks would take Rome; Florence would be destroyed; Bologna, the seat of learning, would be abandoned; Lombardy would be overwhelmed; Venice despoiled. France would be drawn into the conflict. But the Turks, having eaten the apple of discord and reddened it with their own blood, the abbot predicted, would be driven out of Rome and Constantinople, and all Christendom would be restored.

Such a scenario must have been in many minds when in 1565 rumors of a Muslim naval threat to Malta aroused fear throughout Christian Europe. Philip II, son of the Holy Roman Emperor Charles V, ordered that a royal war galley be built as flagship for a counterattack against the Ottoman fleet; this would herald a campaign to recapture Constantinople and liberate the Holy Land. Philip's various titles indicated the monumental stakes involved: King of Spain, Portugal, and the Two Sicilies, Regent of the Netherlands, Duke of Burgundy and Milan, titular sovereign of Jerusalem, heir to the Eastern imperial title conceded to Spain by Byzantium, Emperor of the Indies, Lord of the New World. Philip II was the first monarch to rule on four continents. Christened the *Argo* in reference to Jason's quest for the Golden Fleece and his victory of West over East, the flagship galley bore scenes of the Argonautic journey on its stern. The ship was completed and inspected by Philip in 1570 when, in the spring of that year, Ottoman Sultan Selim II launched a naval offensive in the eastern Mediterranean and raids up the Adriatic coast.

In reaction, a huge Christian flotilla was assembled of ships from Philip II's Spain, the Papal states, and the Venetian Republic Empire: a "Holy League" under the overall command of Don John of Austria. The Ottoman fleet under Ali Pasha met them in October 1571 in the western gulf of Greece near Lepanto. This would be the last great galley (oar-propelled) battle of history as the great barges grappled fast to each other and soldiers fought across their decks as if on land. The Turks were defeated in what long thereafter would be hailed as a decisive moment for Christendom. As one commentator put it, "Sultan Selim II would have been adding minarets to the Basilica of St. Peter in Rome had the Holy League not prevailed at Lepanto."

The profound impact of this battle on the Western psyche and its concern for world order would be displayed during World War I in G. K. Chesterton's battle-song "Lepanto," perhaps the best doggerel poem in English, which featured the fact that Cervantes, later the author of *Don Quixote*, fought at Lepanto:

> Cervantes on his galley sets the sword back in the sheath
> (Don John of Austria rides homeward with a wreath.)
> And he sees across a weary land a straggling road in Spain,
> Up which a lean and foolish knight forever rides in vain,
> And he smiles, but not as Sultans smile, and settles
> back the blade . . .
> (But Don John of Austria rides home from the Crusade.)

Don Quixote, the first modern novel, would be filled with Muslim-Christian episodes and even assert that it was written not by

Cervantes but by "a Moor," Cide Hamete Benengeli. If so, *Don Quixote* would be the first Muslim classic of European literature; but it was not so, only Cervantes' fancy.

Remarkably, the Holy League did not follow up on its victory; there was no attempt to regain lands lost to the Ottomans. Instead, Philip II of Spain turned his forces toward the north, to deal with the challenge from within Christendom. As Chesterton said, "The Reformation was a Christian mutiny during a Muslim invasion." As a result, the world-historian William McNeill wrote, "Despite the Christian victory at Lepanto, the Turks could justly claim an overall success, for they kept at least nominal control of Tunis and Algeria and maintained the naval presence in the eastern Mediterranean they had won from the Venetians in the fifteenth century."

At the opening of the world's modern age, three imperial, highly sophisticated, and militarily mighty Muslim courts—the Ottoman, Safavid, and Mughal—were ruling Turkey, Persia, and India, a huge swath of the known world. At the same time, the eighth-century Sunni–Shia conflict over whether the Prophet's successor should be elected or pass by lineage had reemerged with violence through the conquest of Persia by the Safavids, a Shia dynasty. The Sunni-Shia split would constitute the central feature of Islamic history in the seventeenth and eighteenth centuries. By comparison, the collision with Europe was marginal.

From Europe's perspective, the long genealogy of attitudes toward Islam hardened into the concept of "oriental despotism," primarily produced by face-to-face contacts between the commercially dynamic Venetian Empire, reaching deep into the islands and coasts of the eastern Mediterranean, and the Sublime Porte, the Ottoman court in Constantinople. Venetian agents and ambassadors reported corruption, decadence, and power abuse so extensive that "greater tyranny the world has never seen." Turks became aware that there was no atrocity they would not be accused of. Above all, Venetian ambassadorial dispatches emphasized the Ottoman Empire's fundamental incompatibility with Christendom and the Western system: "the two orders are absolutely at variance with one another." On one side a free population, a hereditary aristocracy, and stable legal institutions. On the other side eradication of the elites of every conquered country and the reduction of all subjects to servitude "such that the entire social body is brought down to a common level of utter indignity." So, from the end of the seventeenth century and throughout the eighteenth, a specter haunted the European idea of order: the specter of oriental despotism. Montesquieu's *The Spirit of Laws*, 1748, would depict the political theories and practices—monarchical and republican—of the West as decisively shaped by Christianity's reaction to its vision of oriental despotism, as evident in the West's rejection of polygamy and its elevation of the idea of womanhood.

THREE WORLD-HISTORICAL EVENTS

The most consequential events affecting the problem of modern world order have been the rise of Islam, global exploration, and Europe's state system.

First came the rise of Islam with its great Arab conquests, which were not only battle victories but also revolutionary repudiations of the Roman and Persian world orders. These were followed by the establishment of an "international" caliphate rule and eventually by a steep decline in Arab-Islamic power.

Second came the reconnaissance and exploration of the globe. Between 1000 and 1500 an Islamic world system flourished across a vast portion of the southern hemisphere. The Indian Ocean and Arabian Sea between India and East Africa were a Muslim lake until the Portuguese expedition under Vasco de Gama rounded the Cape of Good Hope and reached Calicut, India, in 1498. The construction of a string of Portuguese forts along the Arabian-Persian littoral followed and broke the Islamic world trading system. Vivid physical evidence of this emerged from a twentieth-century Oxford University study of the Amiriya at Rada in Yemen, a large madrasa constructed by Sultan Amir ibn Abd al-Wahab around 1500. The building displays unmistakably Indian architectural motifs, revealing a long and well-established seaborne interaction between the Malabar Coast and the Horn of Africa, a cultural-economic system that collapsed not long after the madrasa's completion. During the centuries of Ottoman-Christendom confrontation, European explorers visited most of the habitable regions of the globe, and nearly all those accessible by sea. They found vast territories formerly unknown to them and drew the rough outlines of the world we now know. Europeans thus came to think of all the seas as one and all the world as a whole.

Third was the development of an international state system in Europe in the seventeenth century and its spread and adoption by nations on every continent. This would become a "procedural" system, designed to forestall religious confrontations such as had inflamed the Thirty Years' War.

Today's problem of Islamism and world order is that Islam, the first of the above three world-historical phenomena, has been a uniate and therefore an unsuccessful and, in part, adversarial participant in the pluralistic and procedural third phenomenon.

Recent scholarship has revealed a phenomenon called the Global Renaissance. Commonly seen in recent centuries as only a process of European penetration, exploitation, and domination, these cross-cultural encounters generated material exchanges across varying power relationships and led to a complex cross-pollination of art, culture, beliefs, and technologies. The circulation of goods required the circulation of people who travelled abroad, inserted themselves in foreign communities, and returned with exotic products. Cultural understanding was crucial to successful trade.

In this process, images of Muslims proliferated in a variety of literary and cultural representations. Encounters between West and East began to belie the stereotypes. Actual interactions multiplied and complicated simplistic notions about "the Turk." Travelers' accounts began to combine admiration and sometimes awe with the legacy of demonization.

Out of this age of reconnaissance and renaissance came a great paradox: the recognition that mankind is unimaginably and often intractably diverse. From this reality would emerge an outline of the modern international state system designed to accommodate such diversity in a common understanding of world order.

One of history's great rhetorical events took place in 1550 in Valladolid, Spain, between Bartolomé de las Casas and Juan Ginés de Sepúlveda on whether American Indians were natural slaves of the Spanish. Las Casas prevailed. His view, based on the treatise of Francisco de Vitoria, *On the Indies*, and ratified by the University of Salamanca, determined that Native Americans had souls and were fellow humans, and that conquest of the New World was unjustified on its merits. As Las Casas portrayed them, the conquistadors were no better than cannibals.

Sepúlveda had argued that war against the Indians was justified in order to convert them. Las Casas responded:

> For the Creator of every being has not so despised these peoples of the New World that he willed them to lack reason and made them like brute animals, so that they should be called barbarians, savages, wild men, and brutes, as [the *Sepulvedistas*] think or imagine. On the contrary, they are of such gentleness and decency that they are, more than the other nations of the entire world, supremely fitted and prepared to abandon the worship of idols and to accept, province by province and people by people, the word of God and the preaching of the truth.

This moral argument—based on natural law and inserted into the field of international relations—emerged eventually as a belief in universal human rights, designed to accept and encompass the greatest diversity of the world's peoples.

CHAPTER TWO

The Modern Ordering Takes Shape

T HE CATALYTIC EVENT of the modern order would be the Thirty Years' War, 1618–1648, the most destructive of the wars of religion. Religious and political differences set Catholics against Protestants off and on for three decades. As conflicts multiplied, virtually every major European land became involved directly or indirectly.

The Thirty Years' War marked a transition from feudal to modern warfare. New technologies of killing and the devastation of civilian populations led the Dutch jurist-diplomat Hugo de Groot, called Grotius, to state principles of "law" to govern operations in international combat. Grotius accepted war as a fact of human existence. "Hence both parties to every war are regarded as being in an identical legal position, and consequently as being possessed of equal rights." He assumed that the warring parties would be legitimate states, not governments (governments would change while states remained), each willing to abide by international law as an institution of international society. Not to do so would be "uncivilized."

This was the first expression of the doctrine of the equality
of states, the cornerstone of the international state system. The
state would provide a stable basis of legitimacy beyond religious
allegiance, and in a secular public sphere. Grotius made modern an ancient perception—that the world's diverse peoples are
nonetheless a universal society, a "family of nations" or, as some
say today, an "international community."

Unity and diversity are here joined. The reconnaissance and
exploration of the world had made clear its oneness, while at
the same time making it undeniable that peoples, cultures, religions, and politics were seemingly so disparate as to be almost
irreconcilable.

1648

The Treaty of Westphalia in 1648 brought hostilities to an end.
There is little debate that the Peace of Westphalia was a pivotal
moment. But at the negotiating tables of Münster and Osnabrück
in Westphalia were, as a historian of the treaty put it, "men who
were laboring, each in his own way, for the termination of a
terrible war. They had no idea of progress. The word 'innova-
tion' was anathema to them. The last thing on their minds was
the creation of a new system of sovereign states . . ."

Nonetheless, the modern international state system did grow
from seeds sown at Westphalia. From the fifteenth and sixteenth
centuries' global reconnaissance and exploration came a growing conviction that only procedural arrangements for international interaction could accommodate such a plethora of

peoples, policies, and beliefs. Here was the single most significant idea for world order: the system must be *procedural, not substantive*.

Thus the system required only that its members adhere to a minimal number of practices and procedures which would make it possible for states and other international entities to engage in working relationships even though they might be committed to vastly different, even mutually antagonistic, substantive doctrines and objectives.

The Westphalian agreement pointed to these few basic elements for international relations:

- The Thirty Years' War had been a war of religions. The new international system, while recognizing and respecting all religions and their aims, would expect that religious arguments not be brought to the diplomatic bargaining table.

- The fundamental entity of international relations would be the state—not because of any political or philosophical theory, but simply because the state had proven more responsive and capable than its rival forms of governance in the early modern period, such as empires, city-states, or the Baltic Hanseatic League.

- Norms, laws, and other international understandings would be encouraged. Again, these would not be deductively arrived at from any higher divine source but instead would be based on positive agreements—made and kept solely on the basis that the parties agreed to do so for mutual benefit.

- A process aimed at reducing the horrors of war and facilitating the achievement of peace would be initiated. This would take the form of a responsibility to field professional military and diplomatic services, each with its own set of protocols.

The genius of the Westphalian system, its one big "hedgehog" idea, was that there must be many "foxes," each acting through generally agreed commitments so as to accommodate humanity's diversity. If your state abides by the few requirements, you may follow—bounded by accepted international norms—virtually any substantive policy, including an established religion, and still be recognized as a legitimate member of the international community. This would mean that the international system could *not* accommodate members with ideologies that would impose their substantive beliefs and demands in ways which would override the procedural system.

THE ENLIGHTENMENT VIEWS THE PROPHET

The Enlightenment strengthened, albeit inadvertently, the Westphalian international state system in two ways, both enunciated by Immanuel Kant. First, Kant in his essay "What is Enlightenment?" called upon mankind "to leave its self-caused immaturity" by rejecting "superstition"—in other words, religion and indeed any traditionally accepted source of authority. This would be the Age of Reason, and reason alone would suffice; no more need for revelation (contrast this with Kant's supposed Islamic antithesis al-Ghazali). Second, Kant's immensely influential argument in his essay "Perpetual Peace" provided not substantive but methodological reasons why government by consent of the governed—a republic or a democracy—was essential to world order. It would take at least two hundred years for this added aspect of the system to take hold.

The intellectual tone of the West toward Islam shifted significantly with the Enlightenment. Montesquieu's role was transformative. His *Persian Letters*, 1721, ran through ten editions in one year. But it was not until his *The Spirit of the Laws*, published in 1748, that the West's idea of the East, and of the importance of history itself, changed in a major way. Hugh Trevor-Roper has demonstrated that an important work by Dimitrie Cantemir, prince of Moldavia, *The Growth and Decay of the Ottoman Empire*, was wholly ignored despite being actively promoted when published in London in 1735. But after *The Spirit of the Laws* gave history a sociopolitical dimension of current urgency, that same volume of Ottoman history was read and used later in the eighteenth century by two of Montesquieu's disciples: Edward Gibbon, in his *Decline and Fall of the Roman Empire*, and Sir William Jones, who would become the first of the great "Orientalists." Suddenly the East became intellectually vibrant as a subject for Western study.

Islamic thought became a way to criticize Christianity. Some scholars have gone so far as to place the Enlightenment idea of Islam at the heart of the Enlightenment and make Muhammad the *eminence grise* of the eighteenth century worldview. The *philosophes* found a means of expressing their anti-clericalism and attacking Catholicism by presenting Muhammad as a great

religious figure whose main objectives had been liberty, tolerance, and social justice. Voltaire drew the new boundary line.
After writing his 1721 play *Le Fanatisme on Mahomet le Prophete*
depicting Muhammad as a wicked charlatan, Voltaire in his
Essai sur les Moeurs praised the Prophet as an exemplar of religious tolerance. Enlightenment intellectuals took up this positive theme in as excessive a manner as the medieval denigration
of Islam had been. In *Decline and Fall of the Roman Empire*,
Edward Gibbon's chapter 50 on the life of Muhammad is such
elegant and inspiring prose that it might itself be a sacred text.
His praise for the Prophet and Islam is a not-so-stealthy attack
on Christianity.

If it is possible for any religion to be admired by an Enlightenment savant, Gibbon seems to say, it is Islam, rooted in *reason*:

> The creed of Mohammed is free from suspicion or ambiguity; and
> the Koran is a glorious testimony to the unity of God. The
> prophet of Mecca rejected the worship of idols or men, of stars
> and planets, on the rational principle that whatever rises must be
> set, that whatever is born must die, that whatever is corruptible
> must decay and perish. In the Author of the universe his rational
> enthusiasm confessed and adored an infinite and eternal being,
> without form or place, without issue or similitude, present to our
> most secret thoughts, existing by the necessity of his own nature,
> and deriving from himself all moral and intellectual perfection.
> These sublime truths, thus announced in the language of the
> prophet, are firmly held by his disciples, and defined with meta-
> physical precision by the interpreters of the Koran. A philosophic
> theist might subscribe to the popular creed of the Mohammedans:
> a creed too sublime perhaps for our present faculties.

Gibbon employs Islam as the admirable counter-example to his indictment of Christianity, and he uses "Mahomet" to represent the Muslim state. Here was a religion with a human founder, without monks or priests, which demanded simplicity and resisted complication, organizationally loose, so that human progress would not be obstructed as, Gibbon asserted, the Christian church had done. In sum, Islam was to Gibbon "a model of that judicious blend between rationally demonstrable verity and socially useful prejudice which is the best that can be hoped for in a religion."

Goethe's writings convey a coy infatuation with Islam. *Mahomets Gesang* of 1772 portrays a great creative spiritual leader whose message is described in terms of a stream issuing from a rocky spring to eventually flow into a valley of wealth and beauty. His *West-Östlicher Divan* of 1814 presents poems inspired by the fourteenth-century Persian poet Hafiz, and Goethe depicts himself as a Muslim bard, "Hatem." Fragments remain of a drama, "Mahomet," which apparently never got beyond the planning stage. These intriguing indicators later led some Muslims to regard Goethe as virtually a Believer, rather in the way some Christians saw in Dante's Virgil a Christian before the fact.

A very different Muslim culture is depicted in Mozart's 1781 opera *The Abduction from the Seraglio*, a work that intricately intermingles Enlightenment philosophy, politics, and delight in the exotic. There is barbarous but exciting oriental music, lascivious but adorable conduct, and a despotic but redeemable Pasha. This is not the dreaded Turk of yore. Since the last Ottoman siege of Vienna was broken in 1683, the Turks had ceased to be

considered a real threat to Europe and their empire seemed peren-
nially poised to fall apart. Fittingly, the opera was hurried into
production to be ready for the visit of Grand Duke Paul Petrovich
of Russia, coming to conspire with Emperor Joseph II on a secret
treaty aimed at starting the carve-up of the Ottoman domains. At
the end, Pasha Selim pardons the young (Christian) lovers even
though he has learned that the noble lad is the son of the Pasha's
deadly enemy. Among the Enlightenment themes in the final
resolution are: all humanity as one family; the importance of the
state in securing society; and, as the lovers sing in the closing
scene, "Nothing is so hateful as revenge." Muhammad and Islam
are nowhere to be found in the libretto.

In the United States, Washington Irving, the first internationally recognized American man of letters, was ambassador
to Spain when he wrote *Tales of the Alhambra*, stories of the
long-departed Arab Caliphate of Al-Andalus centered around
its fairy-tale palace set on a rocky spur above Granada.

In 1849 Irving published his big two-volume history-biography
Mahomet and His Successors, which sold well for years. Irving
sought to depict Muhammad as both a God-inspired prophet and
a world-historical figure, consciously rejecting the antipathy of
the pre-Enlightenment West. Irving turned the record over and
over, examining each disparaging accusation and refuting each
in turn as if he were Muhammad's lawyer. As a good Christian,
Irving concludes that Muhammad was an inspired genius, but a
literary—although illiterate—rather than a *religious* genius:

> All the parts of the Koran supposed to have been promulgated
> by him at this time, incoherently as they have come down to us,

and marred as their pristine beauty must be in passing through various hands, are of a pure and elevated character, and breathe poetical, if not religious, inspiration.

A signal change took place, Irving writes, after Muhammad's flight to Medina, when he finds himself revered as the Prophet:

> From this time worldly passions and worldly schemes too often give the impulse to his actions, instead of that visionary enthusiasm which, even if mistaken, threw a glow of piety on his earlier deeds.

Here were the seeds, Irving found, of Islam's swift transformation of the world, but also the sources of its downfall. When the Arab empire pressed too far and was counterattacked, the caliphate of Cordoba was lost in 1031. Little territory was left in Muslim hands except Granada, which fell to the Christian *Reconquista* in 1492.

At the end of the book, however, Irving's admiration for Muhammad seems even greater, not from admiration for the Prophet's victories or the wealth that poured in as spoils of war, but because Muhammad never altered his simplicity of manner and appearance and instead used his wealth to promote the faith and relieve the poor. And throughout it all, "Prayer, that vital duty of Islamism and that infallible purifier of the soul, was his constant practice."

Irving depicts a rising and seemingly irresistible universal monotheistic system of world order under the leadership of the Prophet and caliphate, then its over-reaching and decline. Irving singles out Jesus, not the Prophet, as the divinely inspired

one, yet regards Muhammad as worthy of great praise. Pledged
as an American diplomat to the separation of church and state,
Irving nevertheless fully appreciated the power of religion, and
Islam, in world history. The actual condition of Islam at the
time was otherwise. Only a few years after Irving published his
Mahomet, Herman Melville, author of *Moby Dick,* toured the
Holy Land. In Cairo he saw "the collapse of Islam: ruined
mosques, domes knocked in like stoven boats. Others, upper
part empty and desolate with broken rafters and dismantled
windows; rubbish below, the dirty rites of religion."

The Sick Man of Europe

The invasion and conversion of the Turks produced the
Ottoman Empire, which at its peak was the greatest of all
claimants to world power. But Suleiman the Magnificent's
failure to take Vienna in 1529 appears in retrospect to mark the
high point; from then on, Muslim power ceased to expand. This
came in the midst of the great European reconnaissance of the
world from the fifteenth through the seventeenth centuries. As
one Muslim scholar put it,

> The West and the core of what is now the Islamic World [had
> been] like two separate universes, each preoccupied with its own
> internal affairs, each assuming itself to be the center of human
> history, each living out a different narrative—until the late
> seventeenth century when the two narratives began to intersect.
> At that point, one or the other had to give way because the two
> narratives were crosscurrents to each other. The West being

more powerful, its current prevailed and churned the other one under. But the superseded history never really ended. It kept on flowing beneath the surface, like a riptide, and it is flowing down there still. When you chart the hot spots of today's world—Kashmir, Iraq, Chechnya, the Balkans, Israel and Palestine, Iran—you're staking out the borders of some entity that has vanished from the maps but still thrashes and flails in its effort not to die (Ansary, xxi).

Shift the metaphor and this describes Spengler's pseudomorphosis, a "modern overlay" on Arabian culture, producing a new era of hatred.

The ultimate question addressed in this book is the condition of the modern overlay—the international state system—and the Muslim world's relation to it.

The nineteenth century, with its fixation on nationalism, ethnicity, language, and culture, elevated the Peace of Westphalia into a manifestation of the Divine Plan. As philosopher Georg Wilhelm Friedrich Hegel declared, "It is the way of God with the world that the state exists."

This conviction was amusingly portrayed in a French novel portraying a nineteenth-century village family scene:

'Well,' says Father, 'since you aren't thinking about anything you can tell me the date of the signing of the Peace of Westphalia.'

Antoine neither moved nor answered. His father remonstrated in a shrill voice . . . 'You hear that everyone? He doesn't know the date of the Peace of Westphalia! He ought to be ashamed of himself!'

The carriage was filled with a shocked silence. For her brother's benefit Lucienne mentally recited a prayer recommended by the Desmoiselles Hermeline as an aid to recalling the Great Dates of History. Frédéric drew the figures in the air with his finger, and Mme Haudouin tried to catch her son's eye in order to comfort him with an affectionate smile. But Antoine, staring down at his boots, refused to say anything . . .

Finally, Antoine's breast heaved with a sob . . . He gulped and muttered in a stifled voice: '1648.'

From the early modern period, owing to its geographic proximity to Europe, the Ottoman Empire had been drawn into the Westphalian states-system as a factor in the balance of power. At first, the Ottomans refused to participate formally as full members of international society because, as Bernard Lewis wrote, their sense of "the immeasurable and immutable superiority of their own way of life caused them to despise the barbarous Western infidel from an attitude of correct doctrine reinforced by military power." The Ottomans had accepted embassies from the West but refused to send their own in return, a way to express contempt for Europe.

Beginning with the Enlightenment, and on into the nineteenth century, Christian hostility and Turcophobia were receding owing in large part to the recognition that the Ottomans were no longer the threat they once were thought to be. During this period the Ottomans claimed uniquely expanded sway over Islam even as the political and military powers of the empire were in steep decline.

Throughout most of the first half of the nineteenth century the principal geostrategic issue was whether Russia should be allowed to dismember the Ottoman Empire and control the Turkish Straits which gave access from Russia and Central Europe through the Black Sea and the Dardanelles to the Mediterranean. The answer would be written in blood by the Crimean War of 1854–1856.

In 1850 a dispute had arisen over the keys to certain Christian holy places in Jerusalem. Russia saw it as a French-British-Ottoman threat to its traditional guardianship of Orthodox sites and moved Russian troops into some Ottoman vassal lands in southeast Europe. This was the proximate cause of the Crimean War. The real cause, the diplomatic historian Paul Schroeder wrote, was "the most complicated, persistent, and dangerous question in European politics, the Eastern question." The Tsar saw Turkey falling under the control of western European states, undermining Russia's dominant position in the Black Sea region. Britain and France were determined to block Russian expansion southward. In doing so, as one study put it, "Anglican England and Roman Catholic France were aligned with Islam's sultan-caliph against the tsars." The outcome of the Crimean War would leave Russia humiliated and weakened. What might have become a general European war was confined to Ottoman-Russian territories. The Eastern Question—what would be done to carve up the dying Ottoman Empire—remained unanswered.

From that time forward—long before Sarajevo in 1914—Russia was preparing for war with Ottoman Turkey and all the European powers concerned with control of the Turkish Straits.

This time, Russians were convinced, it would have to be a general European war, a war of empires to answer the Eastern Question once and for all.

The Treaty of Paris in 1856 which concluded the Crimean War began an effort to integrate the Ottomans into the international state system, admitting the empire as a "provisional" member of European and international society. A preliminary to signing was the Sultan's promulgation of a new reform charter guaranteeing the equality of all Ottoman subjects regardless of religious belief. This was, in the Westphalian sense, a "norm" of the system and required of the Ottomans if they were to be accepted as a treaty partner. As a leading scholar of the international system put it, "For many Turks, the wholesale reform of the Ottoman Empire was anathema. It seemed not only a betrayal of the established customs and order, but also a highly visible reminder of concessions made to a foreign standard of 'civilization.' The repugnance Turks felt toward these concessions was proportionate with their sense that the Ottoman Empire lacked viable alternatives." Nonetheless, in a symbolically significant move, the Ottoman Sublime Porte left Topkapi in 1856 to take up residence in the new Dolmabahçe Palace, a European-style edifice suitable for statecraft and diplomacy in the international state system.

The Preamble of the Treaty of Paris declared that the independence and integrity of the Ottoman Empire were necessary for the peace of Europe. The Ottomans thereby were admitted as a participant in the public law of Europe, tentatively recognized as a European state, and guaranteed against expropriation by other states, Russia of most concern. A kind of precursor to

America's "Open Door" policy on China, the treaty was designed to prevent rival European states from warring on each other in order to gain Ottoman lands.

Paradoxically, as its strategic position vis-à-vis Europe was declining, the Ottoman Empire began to assert more religious sway over Islam.

The Ottoman caliphate, not being Arab, claimed its authority directly from God, "to be the vice regent of Allah, not a mere successor of the Prophet." Ottoman conquests by the sword revealed the will of Allah. Accordingly, as early as the eighteenth century, Turkish diplomats when dealing with Christian powers had begun to convey that Ottoman possession of the caliphate implied a religious relationship between the Ottoman sultan and Muslims dwelling beyond Ottoman-ruled lands. The 1774 treaty between Sultan Abdul Hamid I and Catherine II of Russia balanced Catherine's claim to be the patroness of Orthodox Christians living in the Ottoman Empire with a similar claim by the Sultan over Muslims in the Russian Empire. Thus the caliph began to be regarded as something of an equivalent to the pope, as "the Pontiff of the Musulmans," although such a comparison was not grounded in Islamic doctrine. By the late nineteenth century, the extent of the claim of authority of the Ottoman sultan's caliphate stretched far beyond that of the previous generations of Ottoman rule. Sultan Abdul Hamid II had this expanded role inserted in the constitution of 1876, on the eve of the Russian-Ottoman war which would put the term "Sick Man of Europe" into Europe's political vocabulary. By 1878, Russian troops were camped at the foot of Constantinople's walls. The Treaty of Berlin checked

Russian encroachment (Disraeli pledged Britain to defend the Ottoman Empire) but also "was tinctured by the spirit of compromise" as Russia was allowed to appropriate Bessarabia and parts of Armenia. Significantly, the treaty ceded Bosnia-Herzegovina to Austria while Romania, Serbia, Montenegro, and Bulgaria, albeit still under Ottoman "suzerainty," became independent. The Muslim world was profoundly agitated by this news of European encroachment on dominions which had been part of Dar al-Islam. The Europeans saw those same lands of the Balkans and a great stretch of the Mediterranean seaboard as "The Eastern Question." How would they be divided among the European powers?

In reaction, the sultan, emphasizing his broadly-claimed caliphate, sent emissaries to distant Muslim lands—India, China, Java—to declare that Islam's caliphate was still held in Constantinople and to call on all Muslims to rally to the Ottoman standard. It was a moment not unlike, in reverse, Byzantine emperor Manuel II Palaeologus's call on Western Europeans in 1400, and received a like response. Liberal Muslim intellectuals, newly aware of life in the West, sometimes by residence there, were unwilling to support an overweening yet ineffective ruler such as Sultan Abdul Hamid had shown himself to be.

As the "Sick Man" worsened, the "Eastern Question" grew more pressing and European powers reconsidered whether the Ottomans should have been given any place at all in the international state system. The "Young Turk" revolution of 1908 deposed Abdul Hamid. The Sunni Muslim doctrine that the caliph must be of the Prophet's Qurayshi lineage still stuck in the minds of millions. But the Ottoman caliphate's late claim to exercise theocratic authority over all the world's Muslims was considered too valuable to be lightly abandoned by the new constitutional government in Constantinople. The vestigial Abbasid caliphate in sixteenth-century Egypt had shown that it was possible for a caliph to retain the role without a shred of temporal power. So from 1908, the Ottoman Empire was governed by an oligarchic party organization in the name of a puppet Ottoman caliph.

A wholly novel Eastern Question arose after the accession of Wilhelm II to the German throne: whether Germany would, in effect, swallow Turkey whole. Unlike Bismarck, Wilhelm II considered the Near East to be of immense importance. As early as 1889, despite the Iron Chancellor's disapproval, the young kaiser visited Constantinople. When, in 1895, Lord Salisbury secretly proposed to Germany that Turkey ought to be divided among the Great Powers, Wilhelm rejected the idea; he had greater ambitions. Russia was not blind to all this, considering the possession of Constantinople and the Turkish Straits to be a well-settled aim of Russian policy. To block German ambitions, Russian plans were made to seize the Ottoman capital when the next general European war should break out. In 1898, Kaiser Wilhelm toured Palestine, Jerusalem, and Damascus as "Hajji Wilhelm," encouraging the rumor that he was a Muslim who had made the pilgrimage to Mecca.

The widely read statesman-novelist John Buchan's thriller *Greenmantle* places the intrepid British agent Richard Hannay, the South African adventurer Pieter Pienaar, and their strange American friend John Scantlebury Blenkiron in the midst of a cauldron of intrigue in Constantinople, where Ottoman clerks, Islamist fanatics, and German officers and engineers are crammed together in evil-spawning inns.

> There were shouts from the crowd—"*Alleman*" and a word "*Khafiyeh*" constantly repeated. I didn't know what it meant at the time, but now I know that they were after us because we were Boches and spies. There was not love lost between the Constantinople scum and their new masters. It seemed an ironical end for Pieter and me to be done in because we were Boches. And in we should be. I had heard of the East as a good place for people to disappear in; there were no inquisitive newspapers or incorruptible police. I wished to Heaven I had a word of Turkish. But I made my voice heard for a second in a pause of the din, and shouted that we were German sailors who had brought down big guns for Turkey, and were going home next day. I asked them what the devil they thought we had done? I don't know if any fellow there understood German; anyhow, it only brought a pandemonium of cries in which that ominous word *Khafiyeh* was predominant.

The humiliation of Ottoman decline amidst European disdain was a factor in Turkey's decision to ally itself with Imperial Germany in the Great War; indeed, it was Ottoman participation which gave the war recognition as the First *World* War. On September 19, 1914, the Ottoman Empire declared war. The wildest dreams of Imperial Germany were realized, for a moment, in the Near East. On the basis of a *fatwa* by the Sheikh-ul-Islam, the Sultan-Caliph Mehmed V proclaimed a *jihad* on November 14, 1914, a holy war on the side of the kaiser's Germany and against the allied powers of Britain, France, and Russia.

> O Muslims, who are the obedient servants of God! Of those who go to the Jihad for the sake of happiness and salvation of the believers in God's victory, the lot of those who remain alive is felicity, while the rank of those who depart to the new world is martyrdom. In accordance with God's beautiful promise, those who sacrifice their lives to give life to the truth will have honour in this world, and their latter end is paradise.

John Buchan, in *Greenmantle*, vividly conveyed the impact this had in some European minds:

> There is a great stirring in Islam, something moving on the face of the waters. They make no secret of it. And they are quite clear about the details. A seer has arisen of the blood of the Prophet, who will restore the Caliphate to its own glories and Islam to its old purity. His sayings are everywhere in the Muslim world. All the orthodox believers have them by heart. That is why their young men are rolling up to die without complaints in Gallipoli and Transcaucasia. They believe they are on the eve of a great deliverance.

As the historian of the Great War Hew Strachan described it, this *jihadi* call to revolution had the potential to enlist support from across the Muslim world and to inflame anti-colonial movements against European imperial powers, to set

Asia and much of Africa ablaze, forcing the Entente powers to forget the war within Europe as they struggled to hold on to their empires outside it. The message was translated into Arabic, Persian, Urdu and Tatar. It was carried to the Crimea and Kazan, and through Central Asia to Turkestan, Bokhara, Khiva and Afghanistan; it went to India and China; it extended south-east to the Shi'ite Muslims of Iran; and in Africa its call was heard in Nigeria, Uganda, the Sudan, the Congo and as far south as Nyasaland. But its reverberations were minimal. The First World War may have been a war in which men were motivated by big ideas, but that of Islam failed to override the loyalties of temporal rule.

So by the first decade of the twentieth century the great states of Europe had filled the Westphalian state form with imperialism and nationalism; then they went to war with each other. Only in the light of their clashing imperial aims can the significance of the assassination committed on the back street of Sarajevo on June 28, 1914, be understood. To Hew Strachan, "It was an unnecessary war fought in a manner that defied common sense, but on the other hand it was the war that shaped the world in which we still live."

CHAPTER THREE

The Wars on World Order

T O UNDERSTAND the current Islamist assault on world order, it is necessary to recognize that every major war of the modern age has been an ideologically driven attempt—no two alike—to overthrow and replace the Westphalian international state system. Each war would involve, or shed light on, the question of world order and Islamism.

THE FRENCH REVOLUTION AND NAPOLEONIC WARS

Edmund Burke's *Reflections on the Revolution in France* was so titled to indicate that the revolution was an international phenomenon which, while engulfing France at the moment, would soon move outward across the world. Burke predicted, to his everlasting later fame, that the Revolution to overthrow established order would turn to terror until a popular general who possessed the true spirit of command would take charge; the master of the army would become *your* master. That is what happened, with Napoleon Bonaparte declaring, "*I am the Revolution!*"

Hegel saw the French Revolution as the decisive moment in world history: the advent of reason, humanism, and freedom: "The undivided substance of absolute freedom ascends the throne of the world with no power whatsoever in a position to resist it."

Following the young General Napoleon's success in Northern Italy, Bonaparte assessed the prospects for invading Britain and concluded that the French navy could not control the channel. Instead, Napoleon would lead an expeditionary force to Egypt to sever the British link to India, the key to London's world power. Napoleon's ambition was immense. He would take with him a scientific and cultural team—160 strong—of scientists, geographers, orientalists, and artists to expand and transform knowledge of the East. As a man of the Enlightenment, Napoleon genuinely admired the Prophet Mohammad. Using Islamic rhetoric, Napoleon would portray himself as a sultan, declare that France was Muslim, and claim, on behalf of the French Revolution, that France had deposed the pope. He reached out to Tipu Sultan (Fateh ali Khan Shahab, a devout Muslim) in India, proposing an alliance to drive the British from the subcontinent. Napoleon assured the *Directoire* that as soon as he had conquered Egypt, he would move on India.

As Napoleon's *Armée d'Oriente* marched to Cairo, the Ottoman sultan declared jihad against the invader. The Mamluks, Ottoman vassals who were the de facto rulers of Egypt, mobilized under Murad Bey to make a stand at what would be called the Battle of the Pyramids in July 1798. Napoleon's call to his troops,

"Remember that from those monuments forty centuries of history look down upon you," was a theatrical gift to the history books. The Mamluk forces, vastly outnumbered, were crushed. Napoleon, next aiming to lead an Arab revolt against the Turks—a forerunner of Lawrence of Arabia's campaign a century later—moved up the Mediterranean shore to lay siege to the Ottoman bastion at Acre. But Admiral Horatio Nelson sailed in to support the Ottomans and disrupt Napoleon's foray and then turned to the coast of Egypt to destroy the French fleet at the Battle of the Nile. Napoleon's miseries worsened when a plague ravaged his troops. He seized upon news of French setbacks in Europe to return to Paris, leaving his expedition behind.

Napoleon's Egyptian campaign, with its world-spanning ambition for power, had failed. But in cultural affairs it was a triumph, most famously through the discovery of the Rosetta stone by Jean-François Champollion, the Egyptologist who Napoleon had included on his expedition among his team of scholar-experts, his "living encyclopedia," a reference to that keystone of the Enlightenment, Diderot's *Encyclopédie*. For world order, the adventure was, Bernard Lewis concluded, a watershed in history: ". . . the first armed inroad of the modern West into the Middle East, the first shock to Islamic complacency, the first impulse to Westernization and reform. . . . Both parties, in their different ways, learned lessons, drew inferences, and took action."

Napoleon was crowned Emperor of the French in 1804, and in 1806 crushed the Prussian army at the Battle of Jena. Hegel was then a tutor at the University of Jena, in Weimar, working

on his *Phenomenology of the Mind*. As the French army moved
into the town, Hegel heard the clatter of hooves on the cobble-
stones and looked out to see "The Emperor—this world soul—
riding through the city to reconnoitre. . . . an individual who,
here concentrated into a single point, sitting on a horse, reaches
out over the world and dominates it." The French Revolution
may have collapsed after the Terror, but its world-historical
significance would lie in the principle it would impress upon
the world through the idea of "The Great Man." This, in
Hegel's view, would completely transform the established international system. It was "the end of history." Two vast concepts
were joined. From Rousseau, the originator of the revolutionary
idea, came the conviction that all established government was
illegitimate and unjust. From Napoleon, the culminator of the
revolution, came the mastery of the new, centralized state
directed by a universal genius with a universal mission to create
a universal empire. This was a completely new political dispen-
sation, all directed toward universal freedom. The trouble was
that Napoleon by temperament was far more authoritarian
than the monarch overthrown by the Revolution. With the
defeat and final exile of Napoleon in 1815 the French Revolution's immediate threat to the international system was ended,
but its ideology would continue to live in later times and places,
not least in the Middle East.

THE TAIPING REBELLION, 1851–1866

The largest-scale upheaval of violence of the nineteenth century involved the imperial dynasty of Ch'ing China and the

British Empire, then rising toward its peak of world power. This epic contest between two concepts of order was carried out through a massive Chinese rebellion—incited by misunderstood Christianity—against the Ch'ing court and by British determination to force that same Ch'ing court into the Westphalian international system.

Confucian China regarded itself as *the* sole and central world order, entirely self-absorbed, self-sufficient, and superior to all other peoples, whose relationships to the imperial court were properly those of tribute-paying satellites. In stark contrast, the Westphalian system assumed a world of separate states, each one with some degree of juridical equality. The Ottoman Empire and the Ch'ing Empire would take different approaches to the international system.

For China, the conflict focused on trade, which was akin to tribute, heavily regulated and one-sidedly beneficial to China. As long as the West's economic theory was mercantilism, the two approaches to trade had a certain similarity. But after Adam Smith's ideas on free trade took hold, confrontation was unavoidable. British traders began to move up the Chinese coast. When they bought tea and paid in silver, the Chinese saw the inflow as tribute, for China "had no need" to buy British goods. But when the British East India Company began to sell opium to private British merchants who re-sold it in China, demand soared; silver payments began to flow the other way, and the tribute-trade mentality of Imperial China was frontally challenged. An "Opium War" broke out in 1839. Britain seized ports up the coast as far as Shanghai. The 1842 Treaty of Nanking, later denounced as "unequal," forced China to cede five treaty ports to Britain and hand over Hong Kong.

In 1851, a huge rebellion erupted in South China, in large
part made possible by the Opium War's weakening of the Imperial Court. The leader, Hung Hsiu-ch'uan, misinterpreting
evangelical Christian missionaries, declared himself to be Jesus's
younger brother and proclaimed the T'ai-p'ing T'ien-kuo—the
Heavenly Kingdom of Great Peace. His vast peasant army
swept toward the coast and northward, bent on overthrow-
ing and replacing Confucian Chinese rule. This was not just
another in China's age-old series of rural rebellions to reverse
the Mandate of Heaven, but an entirely new, foreign-inspired,
utopian vision of governance. The Taiping Rebellion was the
largest-scale war of the century with an estimated 20 million–
30 million killed.

When the Taipings attacked Shanghai—the West's major
base in China—British and French volunteers, with the support of Imperial Ch'ing troops, repelled the siege, but it would
take several more years to defeat and scatter the rebel forces.
Britain then proceeded to force the weakened court to transform China into conformity with the Westphalian system. In
1856, Lord Elgin was sent to Peking to demand a treaty enabling
Western diplomats to reside in the capital. The Court refused;
to agree would violate China's view of world order. A treaty
and diplomats would place China and Britain on a basis of
state-to-state equivalence within a wholly alien system.

In 1860, Lord Elgin returned to attack Peking, forcing the
emperor to flee the capital. The British then marched north-
west of the city to pillage and burn the Summer Palace. Britain,
on behalf of the international state system, had dragged China
into it; but China was not *of* it. The Boxer Rebellion of 1900,

anti-Christian and anti-foreign, was supported by the vestigial Imperial Court. The Boxer assault was pointedly directed at the foreign diplomatic quarter of the capital, a violent repudiation of the international state system. The American-led Boxer Relief Expedition regained control of the foreign legation district, but China had set itself on a path to become a bitter adversary of the international state system for most of the twentieth century. The three-way conflict among Imperial China, the Taiping Heavenly Kingdom, and the British Empire on behalf of the international system was one of the pivotal wars of world history.

THE AMERICAN CIVIL WAR AND THE UTAH WAR

As the Confucian Chinese Empire sought desperately to repel the Westphalian international system, the Muslim Ottoman Empire was attempting to meet the system's conditions for membership. While the Turks indisputably were part of the European balance of power calculation, they nonetheless were perceived as unable and unwilling to fulfill the international obligation to conform to civilized norms, particularly in their practices of slavery and polygamy. In the mid-nineteenth century, the United States faced a similar problem.

The sixteenth-century great debate on the "humanity" of indigenous New World peoples and the seventeenth-century Westphalian settlement's emphasis on something like "due process" launched a slowly expanding international consensus on the norms required for legitimacy in world affairs. Across the nineteenth century, the two issues of slavery and polygamy gained prominence. Both, as an example, had to be overcome before Siam could meet "the standard of civilization" required for international recognition. King Mongkut, once famed for offering President Lincoln fighting elephants for use in the Civil War, was aware that slavery in his realm was internationally disqualifying. His son Chulalongkorn—Rama IV—declared his subjects to be "free" as of 1868, but did not formally abolish slavery until 1905. Polygamy was personally more difficult; not until 1933 was it made illegal, enabling Siam to "become fully recognized by the world powers as a participant in the Family of Nations as a totally sovereign state . . . within the framework of the legal apparatus of the time."

The American Civil War was "the irrepressible conflict" for several reasons, but one not much recognized was that the United States could not be accepted as an international member state in good standing for so long as it acquiesced in slave-holding within its sovereign borders. Britain outlawed the slave trade in 1807 and in 1833 banned slavery throughout the British Empire. Slavery increasingly was regarded as uncivilized and therefore a bar to equal international dealing among states.

In the post-American Revolution period, the United States held itself somewhat aloof from the international system, regarding it as an arena where undemocratic elites intrigued and plotted for marginal dynastic advantage. The United States determined that it would send no ambassadors abroad and would establish no embassies, employing instead the terms "ministers" and "legations." But these lesser categories increasingly were disadvantageous to the pursuit of America's national interest abroad; the country felt ever greater pressure to get itself clearly accepted by the established world order. The United States, with its South unchanged, could never be regarded as a legitimate international citizen.

Antebellum Southern slaveholders were fully aware that the United States was edging ever-closer to full international involvement and they recognized the hostile context that was creating for their way of life. Yet slavery was inseparable from the South's very identity. For Alexis de Tocqueville, in *Democracy in America* (1835), slavery "was the basic fact destined to exert immense influence on the character, laws, and future of the whole South." Tocqueville makes only sporadic efforts to include the South in his book, then gives up, regarding it as, de facto, another country, beyond the scope of his analysis of America. As the Southern writer Lewis Simpson said: "When the colonial Virginians expediently committed themselves—and the South— to African slavery, they instigated an opposition to modern history that they could not institutionalize within the framework of *their* civilizational tradition." Slavery was therefore central not only to the South's spiritual life but also to its national life: "The South's ideological isolation within an increasingly anti-slavery world was not a stigma or a source of guilt but a badge of righteousness and a foundation for national identity and pride." Thus the South, by its own lights, seemed to have no alternative but to offer the first American resistance to the idea of the modern state in the international system.

When the South seceded to become the Confederate States of America, it immediately sought international diplomatic recognition as a legitimate state. From the intense Civil War diplomatic maneuvering among the United States, Britain, and the CSA described at the heart of the autobiographical *The Education of Henry Adams*, the South surely would have won such recognition were it not for slavery. The British dealt a severe blow to the Union by recognizing the South as a "belligerent," a legal category of international law. But despite the immensely tempting prospect of wrecking the United States permanently, the British would not take that further, final step. The South then resolved to give all-out war to the established international state system and its anti-slavery norm.

At the same time, the rise of a Mormon polity, notorious for its polygamy, presented the United States with a similar international problem. By 1840, the Latter-day Saints had organized themselves as a militia, a theocracy, and a state within a state, its founder Joseph Smith acquiring an international reputation. An 1841 editorial in James Gordon Bennett's *New York Tribune* compared Smith to Muhammad and the Mormons to Islam: "[Smith's] ambition is to found a religious empire that will reach the uttermost ends of the earth." Smith had dispatched what appeared to be ambassadors to European states, as though the Nauvoo polity was itself a sovereign state. In the presidential election of 1856, the Republican Party platform pledged "to prohibit in the territories those twin relics of barbarism: polygamy and slavery." In 1857, a U.S. expeditionary army under Colonel Albert Sydney Johnston marched to confront the large and experienced Mormon militia of Brigham Young in what would be called the Utah War. In 1862, Congress passed antibigamy legislation directed at the Mormons who, in 1890, declared an end to plural marriage at the same time that the

United States was emerging as an accepted power on the world scene and agreeing at last to send and receive resident ambassadors within the Westphalian international system.

In contrast, the 1907 Second Hague Conference continued to consider the Ottoman legal system—shadowed by charges of accepting polygamy and slavery—as less than fully civilized, and the countries attending brushed aside Ottoman diplomatic displeasure at being ranked among the second-class powers at the conference.

THE FRANCO-PRUSSIAN WAR, 1870–1871

Napoleon's defeat, by the "United Nations" in Lord Byron's term, brought two major international developments. The 1814 Congress of Vienna produced a European "conference" or balance-of-power structure which would be praised for keeping the peace for a hundred years, 1814 to 1914. And the victory provided the rulers of Europe with the perfect, anti-revolutionary opportunity to refill the vessel of the Westphalian state with the content of dynastic imperialism, a strategy which had been begun by Louis XIV and succeeded until the coming of the French Revolution.

But the hundred years of peace were viciously interrupted by the Franco-Prussian War of 1870–71. The war can be seen today as an attack on the Westphalian system by the ruling dynasties of the continent, with horrendous consequences for producing the world wars of the twentieth century. And the war produced a communist revolution of "the masses" which would make an equally terrible contribution to world conflict in the century ahead.

Germany, which paradoxically did not emerge from the Thirty Years' War and the Peace of Westphalia as a state but as an agglomeration of hundreds of small political entities, finally achieved statehood through the national unity Bismarck drummed up by way of the war. But it would be an *imperial* state. Bismarck seized the opportunity presented by the question of who would succeed to the Spanish throne to alarm France with the fear that Germany might be planning to revive the Holy Roman Empire as a Protestant realm. French aristo-cratic dread over such a prospect lurks in the background of Henry James' novel, set in 1869, *The American.*

By insidiously re-wording a diplomatic dispatch which would become famous in the literature of international stratagems, Bismarck lured the French into a verbal trap. Insulted, they mobilized for war. The Prussian Army quickly routed the forces of Napoleon III. In January 1871, in the Hall of Mirrors at Versailles, Bismarck had King Wilhelm I of Prussia declared the German Emperor, the *Kaiser.* As the world historian William McNeill wrote, the Franco-Prussian War "led to the unification of Germany, not by the People under liberal leaders but by Prince Otto von Bismarck and the Prussian army . . . Chancellor Bismarck showed how it was possible to strengthen the power of kings and emperors, and other holdovers from Europe's Old Regime, by the very devices and instruments which had been the liberals' most reliable source of strength." Bismarck and the kaiser's new imperial Germany would constitute the Second Reich, the First Reich having been the Holy Roman Empire under Charlemagne, or, Germanically, Karl der Grosse.

The Franco-Prussian War would be the first test of a new movement—launched by the Swiss Henri Dunant after witnessing the horrors of the Battle of Solferino—to tighten the laws of war to provide greater protections for civilians, wounded soldiers, and prisoners of war. Central to this would be greater commitment to professional military standards: wearing uniforms, bearing arms openly, serving under legitimate state authority. The French in 1870, however, deployed *francs-tireurs* (free shooters)—irregular, guerrilla-style, non-professional fighters. Here was the emergence of what in the post 9/11 War on Terror would be recognized as "asymmetrical warfare" involving "illegal combatants." The *francs-tireurs* were reviled as murderers and cowards, hiding amidst civilian populations; by putting themselves outside the professional armed services, they were to get no protections for the new movement begun by Dunant. If caught on the battlefield, they could be summarily executed. In the twenty-first century's Islamist wars, such illegal combatants would be afforded much the same protections as professionals, an upside-down attitude toward the original concept for the laws of war and one which would severely disadvantage, and demean, professional soldiers.

The Commune of 1871 erupted after the Prussian victory when the Paris militia forced the government to flee the city, enabling "the masses" to seize control of the capital. The American minister (i.e., ambassador) Elihu Washburne was

the only diplomat to remain in the city amidst scenes of car-
nage, squalor, and "red flags everywhere." Marxist-Leninists
and, later, Maoists would see in the Paris Commune the birth
of the "Communist Internationale" (the anthem of communism was composed in Paris in 1871), the moment of pure
radical revolution to be emulated thereafter by the workers of
the world.

Thus at Paris in 1870–71 the international state system was
ravaged from both sides of the political spectrum: from the
landed aristocracy of Prussia and from the urban proletariat of
Paris.

The consequences of the war would reshape world order for
the next century. France would no longer be feared as the primary military power in the lineage of Napoleon Bonaparte.
Germany, now united, would march to the forefront of Europe.
International communism could now point to the Paris Commune as a model for Marx's "true" revolution. (The French
Revolution, Marx complained, had been only political, not
the entire transformation of human nature called for in his
Communist Manifesto.)

Europe's relation to Islam also would be altered. In the earlier
nineteenth century, Germany, still fragmented, did not follow
the European colonialist pattern. But in 1872, the Ottomans
requested German engineering advice for a Turkish railway
system. By 1892, a German railroad had reached Ankara. This
would become the "Berlin to Baghdad" Railway, designed
to provide Germany with access to Mesopotamia's oil and
Persian Gulf ports. This would set the stage for what we have
seen to be the long run-up to World War I.

THE GREAT WAR

T. E. Lawrence (of Arabia), a British agent, organized the Arab Revolt under Sharif Hussein of Mecca against the Ottoman Empire. Lawrence participated in raids on the Damascus-Medina railway and entered Damascus, or claimed to have done so, with Arab forces in October 1918. Lawrence, who never disguised his Christianity, gives no indication in his book *Seven Pillars of Wisdom* that Islamic religious fervor played a part in the Arab cause.

As a member of the British delegation at the 1919 Paris Peace Conference, Lawrence conveyed remorse at the way the Arab Revolt had begun on false pretenses: the British promise of support for fully independent Arab nationalism. A secret exchange of notes in 1916 among Britain, France, and Russia outlined their plan for the post-war partition of the Ottoman Empire. Named the Sykes-Picot Agreement for the chief British and French negotiators, this plan called for the Arabian Peninsula to become independent, while trans-Jordan Palestine would be under international control. A French zone would run from the coast of Lebanon through Syria and into Iraq. A British sphere would cover Palestine west of the Jordan River and include the Negev desert. The British would also control central Mesopotamia and the Persian Gulf. The underlying idea was that Britain and France would guide the Arabs toward statehood while gaining economic privileges. Russia agreed with the plan in return for rights in Anatolia and Armenia.

In November 1917 the Bolshevik revolutionaries discovered the secret text in the Russian Foreign Ministry and made it public, denouncing it. Both Arab and Zionist nationalists condemned the Sykes-Picot papers as contrary to promises made in the 1915 McMahon-Hussein correspondence and the 1917 Balfour Declaration of British support for the establishment in Palestine of a national home for the Jewish people.

A map of the Middle East at the end of World War I shows no reference to the Ottoman Empire and indeed no political boundaries at all. The final disposition of Ottoman territories partially reflected the Sykes-Picot agreement, but was modified by a League of Nations mandate system which gave the Allied powers no formal possessions while placing them in de facto authority. Palestine was placed under the British mandate. On this basis the international system, led primarily by Britain and France, began the process of bringing the Middle East into the Westphalian state system, something the Ottoman Empire had sought but which only its collapse could achieve.

The German Reich, with the Ottoman Empire in association, had fought the British, French, and Russian empires, but it mainly had been Germany versus Britain. For the British it had been a war to preserve their island state and its far-flung empire; they were defending a legacy. For the Germans it had been a war to break out of the imposition of a world order by a Pax Britannica and France's *mission civilisatrice*. For Germans the war was not about territory but, as Canadian historian Modris Eksteins said, about *Geist*, spirit. War was "a life-giving principle," an expression of "superior culture," essential to the nation's image and identity.

Grinding trench warfare would put an end to such dreams and an end—almost—to imperialism as a political theory for the modern state system.

Out of the First World War three new ideas would arise to profoundly affect world order in the twentieth century: the reality of a new and dysfunctional Middle East emerging from the ruined Ottoman Empire; the 1917 Bolshevik Revolution which on the corpse of the Tsarist Empire would seek by world revolution to build "the New Socialist Order" led by "the international proletariat"; and the idea of the United States of America itself which, as it entered the war in 1917, by the same step came onto the international scene as a fully Westphalian-style state. From 1898 until the Great War, the United States had been tempted to join the club of territorial world empires. But after the painful experience of the Filipino insurrection, it began to see world power as best exercised in other forms.

As the United States entered the war, Wilson sent his closest adviser, Colonel Edward House, to Europe to urge the allies to make a joint statement of war aims. But House was rebuffed by both the British and French, so work was begun in Washington to draft an American statement to which the whole international community might subscribe. This would be the "Fourteen Points," the single most influential document in American diplomatic history. It was Wilson's analysis of the fundamental causes of modern war and the specific changes necessary for peace.

In sum, the American program was a revitalization of the procedurally based Westphalian state system, in four major ways:

- It laid a basis for rejecting imperialism.
- It proposed a world organization—the League of Nations—which would be the mechanism of its member states for the maintenance of world order.

- It declared the right of "self-determination" under which "a people" or "a nation" could participate in international affairs as a state.
- And—putting into effect Kant's vision in "Perpetual Peace"—it enlisted democracy in the cause of world order, not so much as a "right," but as a procedural necessity for political and economic success.

Wilson put theory into practice. When in 1918 Imperial Germany sought to open talks on an armistice, Wilson refused to agree until the kaiser abdicated and the Second Reich handed over the government to a republic. This was done.

When Wilson's liner *George Washington* landed in France in December 1918, the French Press hailed him as "the incarnation of the hope of the future." As the world historian H. G. Wells described it, "For a brief interval, Wilson stood alone for mankind, And in that brief interval there was a very extraordinary and significant wave of response to him throughout the earth . . . he ceased to be a common statesman: he became a messiah." But ecstatic hope soon turned to bitter disappointment.

At Versailles in 1919, the Allies drew up a settlement that promised far more than they could deliver; they sought solutions which would regulate the affairs not just of Europe but the whole world, under the belief that liberal democracy should be the basis for cooperative progress.

The story of Wilson's inability to carry through with his grand plan is one of the tragic epics in the history of world affairs. But his idealism became a beacon for liberal internationalism ever after.

World War I started when imperialism was at the peak of its power and ended with that form of governance on its way out.

The Ottoman Empire having lost its jihadist war on the side of the kaiser's Germany, the Grand National Assembly on November 1, 1922, declared that the office of the Sultan of Turkey had ceased to exist and that the government had become a republic. Sultan Mehmet VI was deposed and his cousin Abdul Majid Effendi elected as caliph of all Muslims. He was invested with the Mantle of the Prophet, but lacked the power of Ottoman rule. Thus the new caliph was neither a Qurayshi nor possessed of authority as "the sword of Islam."

On March 3, 1924, the caliphate was abolished altogether and the holder of the title exiled to Switzerland. A last attempt to save the Ottoman caliphate was made by Muslim notables of India on the ground that no definite decision on the status of the office should be made without consultations across the entire Islamic world. Failing in their rescue effort, the Indians called for the question of the caliphate to be referred to an international congress of doctors of Islamic law.

Arnold Toynbee, in a special volume on "The Collapse of the Caliphate" for his 1924 annual world survey published by the British Institute of International Affairs, wrote, "If the Muslim community in India were confounded by the abolition of the Ottoman Caliphate, their *bête noir* King Hussayn of the Hijaz was likewise placed in a difficult predicament by the same event." Calls for recovering the caliphate for the Arabs and the Quraysh were raised, for proclaiming King Hussein, who was Sharif of Mecca, as caliph. This provoked Egypt, which saw an opportunity to regain the primacy of the Arab world that it had held prior to the rise of the Ottoman Empire. The idea of Hussein as caliph was rejected by Egypt and India in favor of holding an Islamic Caliphate Congress. Despite this, Hussayn declared himself caliph, a short-lived claim as he had failed to line up widely based Islamic support.

The intrigues and stratagems which followed were untangled by Elie Kedourie in his classic work, *The Chatham House Version.* The idea of vesting the caliphate in King Hussein of the Hijaz had come from Sir Reginald Wingate, British governor-general in Cairo, who had been canvassing Muslim opinion about it since early in the war. Muhammad Mustafa al-Maraghi, chief *qadi*, or judge, of the Anglo-Egyptian Sudan, wrote to Wingate purporting to set out authoritative Muslim doctrine on the caliphate. He threw doubt on the contention—highly favorable to Hussein—that a caliph had to be descended from the Prophet's tribe of Quraysh. The Ottoman caliphate had been recognized by the whole Muslim world, proof that rule by the sword was legitimately the will of Allah. Maraghi was special-pleading, laying the groundwork for a claim to the caliphate by Egypt's King Fuad.

The congress to choose the next caliph met in Cairo in May 1926. Support arose for Ibn Saud, whose forces had recently conquered the Hijaz, deposed King Hussein, and soon would declare the territory he had controlled to be part of the Kingdom of Saudi Arabia. A declaration arrived from Cairo's al-Azhar, the principal institution of learning of Sunni Islam, stating that Egypt was not fit to become the seat of the caliphate. The congress ended as a fiasco, with no decision made. Egyptian and Saudi rivalry had created a bristling stalemate.

From this, two world-historical consequences followed. First, the collapse of the Ottoman Empire and Caliphate left the Middle East without the general Islamic governance presumed under the Quran and Hadith. To fill the vacuum, the Western European victors of the First World War dropped a grid of states, or League of Nations mandates designed to produce states, upon the entire region, bringing it suddenly and problematically into the Westphalian international state system. Second, Islamists regarded 1924 as a catastrophic loss of their divinely authorized world-system of governance, and the region's entrance into the international state system as an abomination to the faith. They would begin planning to repulse, oust, and ultimately destroy the infidel system and replace it with Islamism, a radicalized amalgam of the faith, using the tactic of terrorism. An "Islamist War on World Order" begins at this point.

The world order in question would be the Westphalian international system, now indisputably centered on the state and with a rising America promoting open trade, a public sphere for freedom of expression, and the idea that sovereignty comes from the people, i.e., democracy. Against this, atavistic imperialism rose again.

WORLD WAR II: IMPERIAL JAPAN AND THE THIRD REICH

Numberless studies of the Second World War seem to have explored every dimension of that conflict except one: what

Imperial Japan and the Third Reich really planned to do with the international system. Both of these empires had a well-defined world strategy intended to destroy and supplant the Westphalian state structure.

Japan's aggressions were in the service of a drive to create an "East Asian Co-Prosperity Sphere" in order to secure the natural resources, e.g., oil and rubber, needed for a relatively small island state to become a major industrial world power. Beginning with the Meiji Restoration in 1868, Japan, alone among non-Western nations, urgently and assiduously met every test required to gain acceptance by Westphalian standards of civilization in war, diplomacy, and peace. In sharp contrast to China's unceasing efforts to fend off the outside world and preserve Confucian tradition, Japan as early as 1899 had conformed its governmental institutions, legal system, and diplomatic practices to international requirements. Japan then demonstrated its arrival as a world power by its lightning-quick victory in the Russo-Japanese War of 1904 and its diplomatic sophistication in peacemaking to produce the 1905 Treaty of Portsmouth.

At the same time, Japan did not regard itself as an equal or accepted member of international society, and by the 1912 end of the Meiji Restoration considered itself, as the Japan scholar Edwin Reischauer put it, "almost a different species of animal from the rest of humanity." Emperor Hirohito was enthroned in 1926 as the chief Shinto priest and lineal descendent of the sun goddess Amiteratsu, the divine ruler of the *Kokutai*, the "eternal and immutable polity." Japan was anything but a Westphalian state.

The 1929 world economic crash discredited the West, the free market, and democracy. China's chaotic weakness was seen in Tokyo as an opportunity which had to be seized.

As the magisterial work on Hirohito by Herbert Bix makes clear, Japan's armed forces were under the emperor's command prior and superior to his power over governmental affairs. The emperor-led military was the medium through which the gods worked their will, and *ko do*, the imperial way, was an ideology to liberate Japan from democracy, liberalism, individualism, communism, and all the "isms" of the modern world. It was a "holy war" against the non-Japanese world, a divine mission—certified by victory in 1904—to rule all Asia.

The mission would be carried out under a semblance of respect for international structures. When in 1931 Japan's army invaded Manchuria, it did so under a ruse that might make the move seem justifiable internationally. Japan then invented "Manchukuo" and called for its recognition as a legitimate state. When the scheme did not work, Japan dropped the pretense and canceled its status as a member state of the League of Nations.

Although "East Asian Co-Prosperity Sphere" sounded like an association of states, within Japan's own councils it was made clear that co-prosperity "by no means ignores the fact that Japan was created by the gods or posits an automatic equality." Japan's grand strategy was to create by force a "New Order of East Asia" led by Japanese as the superior race among Asians, themselves a superior race to the rest of humanity. As only German victory in Europe would enable Japan to make major gains in Asia, Japan in 1936 signed the Axis treaty with Nazi Germany and Fascist Italy. Japan's longer term vision was to see the international state system transformed into a three-sphere world order. If America would accept German rule of Europe and Japanese rule of Asia, the Axis would recognize U.S. rule of the Western Hemisphere. The Arab-Islamic Middle East would fall under Germany's sphere of influence.

The groaning shelves of historical scholarship on Hitler's Germany would seem to leave nothing more to say: Europe was savaged by a megalomaniac fixated on the eradication of the Jews. Yet, as with Hirohito's Japan, Hitler's grand strategy has not received much attention. In many ways it mirrored that of Imperial Japan: racially driven, divinely authorized, and designed to do away with the established international order.

A telling moment came in the crisis over Danzig. Formerly the provincial capital of Germany's East Prussia, the post-World War I Treaty of Versailles made Danzig an independent "free city" by authority of the League of Nations. By 1935, the rise of the Nazi Party had the city in peril. Danzig's city fathers took their case to the International Court of Justice in the Hague, arguing that the Nazis were in violation of fundamental international law. Specifically, the principle of *nulla poena sine lege*—no punishment without a law—had been discarded by the Nazis who instead were imposing *nullum crimen sine poena*—no crime without a punishment. This in effect banished law altogether, for now the Party, at will, would decide when and by whom a crime had been committed; it was a re-crossing of the line between might makes right, and "from status to contract," that demarcated the beginning of civilization, a line recognized as far back as Aeschylus's ancient Greek drama, the *Oresteia*. The World Court found for the City of Danzig. The Nazis, of course, sneered at the court's decision. It was Hitler's demand for the return of Danzig to the German Reich that led to Germany's invasion of Poland in 1939 and thus to the Second World War.

Nazi ideology was atavistic: rooted in a mythical, pre-civilizational, supposedly Aryan past. It was millenarian: an empire to last for a thousand years. It was paranoid: rooted in the "Protocols of the Elders of Zion," it felt an imperative to destroy a world Jewish conspiracy. And it was apocalyptic and eschatological, as conveyed in the German-language list of "final" concepts: *Endreich*, *Endkampf*, *Endsieg*, and *Endlösing*, all to produce a New Age, history's climactic Third Status.

Hitler's strategy was specific. The immediate danger to the Reich came from the communist East. *The Nationalsozialistische Deutsche Arbeiterpartei*, National Socialist German Worker's (Nazi) Party, had been formed to lure the working class away from international communism. The communist source of authority in "the People" was to be countered by the Nazi Party's *Das Volk*.

Hitler's Germany therefore was not a state; it was an organic community of the master race. As a living, growing organism, state borders did not apply to Germany. Hitler was precise, emphasizing that he was not a *Grenzpolitiker*, aiming at recovering lost German lands, but a *Raumpolitiker*, driving for the "space" needed for the German race. The international state system, through the despised League of Nations, had created a "small state mess" (*Kleinstatten Gerümpel*) in Eastern Europe which would have to be done away with to gain space for the German people to acquire the *Lebensraum* they needed for their

organic growth to ever more greatness. The outcome would
not be anything resembling a collection of states or a "United
States of Europe," but the *Heerführer Europas*: a German-led
New European Order. Hitler's military might was to be used
not to restore Germany to the place it had held in 1914 but to
overturn the international state system as it existed. Hitler
would sign his new world order into being, he said, at Münster
in Westphalia, to mark the end of the 1648 Westphalian state
system.

Great attention has been given to the role of Hajj Amin
al-Husseini, the British-appointed Grand Mufti of Jerusalem,
in 1939 in support of nationalist-socialist pro-German military
officers of the Syrian and Iraqi Ba'ath movement and in 1941
in proposing an Arab role in Hitler's war against the Jews. In
the context of Field Marshall Erwin Rommel's 1941 drive into
Egypt causing panic among British officials in Cairo, the prospects for German-Arab collaboration on the future of the
Middle East seemed bright. The mufti's meeting with Hitler in
Berlin in November 1941 appeared to produce a confidential
agreement on the ultimate aim of destroying "the Jewish element
residing in the Arab sphere."

Hitler's war against the Jews would culminate in the Holocaust,
which erroneously has been called the reason for the establishment of the modern State of Israel. From antiquity on, Jews
were never absent from the land, and the modern movement
for Jewish nationhood in the Middle East began well back in
the nineteenth century and produced the pre-state *Yishuv*, or
Jewish political community. For this book's purpose, the major
factors are these: First, the founders of the modern State of Israel

understood and were fully committed to the Westphalian international state system. Second, they employed diplomacy and
strength in tandem toward the goal of internationally recognized statehood, and in doing so fielded immensely capable
professional diplomatic and military services in accordance with
the system's requirements. Third, Israelis accepted the requisite
norms: religious tolerance, women's rights, and democratic
political practices. Fourth, all these factors came together during
a "window of opportunity" for new state-making which arose in
the immediate post-World War II years and succeeded in winning
diplomatic recognition—most notably by President Truman's
decision in 1948—and acceptance as a legitimate, sovereign
Member State of the United Nations.

Thus Hitler's grand design to overturn the established world
order was destroyed, even as Israel's commitment to it was ratified. Recent scholarship has portrayed Grand Mufti Hajj Amin
al-Husseini as weak and ineffectual, and Arab support for the
Nazis in the 1930s and 1940s as confined only to the more
extreme elements of the Arab world. But today's Arab media
culture is drenched in Nazi-style anti-Semitism; in retrospect,
the mufti's role as Hitler's propagandist broadcasting shortwave
radio harangues to the Middle East during World War II war-
rants indicting him as an accessory to Hitler's goal of eradicating the Jews for all time.

Beyond their common aim of eradicating the Jews, Nazism
and Islamism were each committed to a single all-encompassing
ideology virulently hostile to the international system's procedurally based acceptance of multifariousness in thought and
practice among its members.

The Cold War

The Axis Pact signed by Germany, Japan, and Italy was directed against the Soviet "Comintern," the Communist International. The American-led Allied victory in World War II, fought in significant part in defense of the international state system, eliminated the Axis challenge but left the United States facing its wartime ally, the USSR, which would pose the latest, and ideologically most comprehensive, danger to the system—now becoming known as the free world. Henry Kissinger described the threat:

> Nothing remotely resembling the Soviet Union had appeared on the horizon of European diplomacy since the French Revolution. For the first time in over a century, a country had dedicated itself officially to overthrowing the established order. The French revolutionaries had striven to change the character of the state; the Bolsheviks, going a step further, proposed to abolish the state altogether. Once the state had withered away, in Lenin's phrase, there would be no need for diplomacy or foreign policy. . . .
>
> Since after a few months or years the state was expected to disappear altogether, the principal task of early Soviet foreign policy was believed to be the encouragement of world revolution, not the management of relations among states.

Communist ideology specifically rejected every core principle of the Westphalian system.

Marxism-Leninism dictated that:

- The state must be smashed. If, after the revolution, the party had need for the state, it would soon "wither away."

- International law and diplomacy were tools of the oppressive capitalist class and had no legitimacy. Their procedures would be used against them.
- The norms of political and civil liberties were invalid; economic and social progress to change human nature was the goal.
- International organizations were arenas for infiltration and takeover by pro-Communist elements.

Under Stalin and his successors, the Soviet Union and other Communist powers engaged with the international state system and professed to adhere to it, including fielding professional military, and diplomatic services. But at the same time, the USSR, People's Republic of China, and their satellites worked to subvert the international system and its leading member states in America and Europe while using terrorist and guerrilla tactics to gain the Third World for the Communist International.

The prolonged period of acute and dangerous hostility between the West and the Soviet Union itself became a kind of international system, marked by crisis management to prevent thermonuclear war, adversarial alliance blocs, a doctrine of deterrence founded on "mutually assured destruction," and enhanced propaganda, subversion, and intelligence collection techniques.

The dangerously immediate threats of the cold war were carried out on two levels: (1) the global strategic nuclear contest; and (2) regional wars waged directly or by proxies in the Third World. The two levels came together most visibly across the decades of the Arab-Israeli conflict. The United States became Israel's big power supporter; the Soviet Union constantly scanned the Middle East for opportunities to thwart steps toward peace and foment trouble for America. The Arab nations, all nominally legitimate state members of the international system, were dominated by military regimes, hereditary monarchies, and, here and there, falsely labeled parliamentary governments run by entrenched elites.

Across the cold war decades the contest vividly displayed itself through that core principle of Westphalia—diplomacy. As described in the biography of the British ambassador to the Sublime Porte of the Ottoman Empire from 1842 to 1852, Viscount Sir Stratford Canning:

> Theoretically, a Moslem could never treat with an infidel—the despised *giaour*—as an equal; yet it was necessary to find some method of dealing with the Europeans, especially as Ottoman power began to decline. . . . the dragoman was the ideal answer . . . the endless possibilities for using up time in sending the dragoman back and forth from embassy to porte with official exchanges, while a word was changed here or a phrase there, was a method they found most appealing . . . Canning learned a first principle of Ottoman diplomacy, namely, that the Turks would delay decision for as long as the other party would tolerate delay, and that they respected people dealing from a position of strength far more than they respected those imbued with tolerance and good will.

The Soviets realized that they could exploit Arab discontent with the state system. To counter this, the United States turned to the system's core function—diplomacy.

Colonel Gamal Abdel Nasser took power in Egypt in the 1950s, declared himself leader of the Arab world, and began to threaten "reactionary" regimes in the name of a militaristic pan-Arab national socialism. The Soviets saw Nasser as an ideal vehicle for cold war troublemaking. In 1962 a colonel's revolt in Yemen's capital of Sana'a sparked a civil war. Egypt intervened with over 20,000 Soviet-equipped combat troops. Saudi Arabia countered with military support for the ousted Yemeni royalists. Nasser ordered Egyptian air strikes on Saudi border towns. All this was taking place as the Cuban missile crisis transfixed the Kennedy White House. American Ambassador Ellsworth Bunker would "invent" shuttle diplomacy, flying back and forth from one Arab capital to another in his personally designated DC-4. Through an exquisite combination of stern-ness and cordiality, Bunker gained agreement for a mutual Egyptian-Saudi withdrawal followed by the arrival of a United Nations Observation Mission.

American shuttle diplomacy became world-famous when Kissinger "shuttled" during the Yom Kippur War between Jerusalem, Cairo, Damascus, and other Arab points on a plane called the "Yo-yo Express" because it went up and down so much. By the end of 1975, Kissinger had persuaded Israel to withdraw for the first time from land gained militarily and Egypt to recognize Israel's right to exist. Kissinger also negotiated an Israel-Syria disengagement agreement on the Golan Heights and mutual acceptance of a United Nations Truce Supervision Operation on the Golan. Both the Bunker and the Kissinger missions were striking achievements by the United States on behalf of the international state system and its world organization, the

United Nations. But Syria, with extensive Soviet support, would become the diehard enemy of the Arab-Israeli peace.

An even more dramatic breakthrough came in the Camp David Accords negotiated in 1978 by President Jimmy Carter, who brilliantly compressed shuttle diplomacy into the forested cabins in Maryland's Catoctin Mountain Park. The result was a complex, carefully drawn document which gained state-to-state recognition for Israel and Egypt and an Arab state negotiating role with Israel on behalf of the Palestinians toward their objective of statehood. No diplomatic achievement could more vividly display the strengths of the international system than this, but the United Nations disgraced itself by refusing to acknowledge the Egypt-Israel Treaty of Peace and refusing to provide a peace-keeping operation for the Sinai. Thus was the international system betrayed from within by its own U.N. organization even as the legitimacy of the state, Israeli or Palestinian, was denounced by rejectionist regimes and Islamist radicals and threatened by new waves of terrorist attacks.

The vicissitudes of cold war-era diplomacy were on display in the strange story of Iran, heir to the ancient empire of Persia, which maneuvered its way through the troubles of the twentieth century—colonial exploitation, war, revolution, and geostrategic partnerships—to be in, but never of, the international system.

Imperial Persia had been divided as early as 1907 into Russian and British spheres of influence for the exploitation of oil reserves. A coup in 1921 by Reza Khan, an army officer, ousted the shah. Reza took the throne himself and began reforms aimed at creating a modern state, including abolition of the veil and cancellation of foreign concessions. In 1935, influenced by his ambassador to Hitler's Germany, Reza adopted the name "Iran," a cognate of Aryan. The name change conveyed recognition of German scholars' theory that a primeval Indo-European culture of Aryan peoples had originated in the vicinity of Persia.

Entangled in World War II resource pressures, Reza abdicated in 1941 in favor of his son Muhammed Reza Pahlavi. With the aid of British and American intelligence services, the Shah fended off leftist, nationalist, and constitutionalist movements to increasingly strengthen his monarchy as a modern inheritor of the ancient Persian Empire and its ceremonial capital of Persepolis.

In June 1964 the American embassy in Tehran sent a long dispatch (A-702 SECRET) on the "Intangible Factors" of Iranian politics. Drafted by Martin Herz, a cold-war-era Foreign Service intellectual of exceptional acumen, the report depicted a hollow shell: "Something is wrong. Something is missing." What is its ideology? What is holding it up? How long can it last? Herz seemed to echo Gertrude Stein's "There's no there there." Only the security service SAVAK and the opposition's apparent inability to conceive of an alternative regime kept the shah in power. The most important "intangible," the dispatch concluded, was the mystique of his imperial institution.

In that same year of Martin Herz's report to the State Department, 1964, the shah forced the Ayatollah Khomeini into exile. The shah then proceeded to make his own "mystique" even more grandiose through world-wide invitations to a gargantuan party in Persepolis to celebrate the 2,500th anniversary of the Iranian nation—and himself as the direct heir of Cyrus the Great. As a Western scholar-invitee wrote, "What we are dealing with is, quite simply, the theory of the Divine Right of Kings as slightly modified by the Persian Constitution of 1906" (a document that significantly shrank the power of the leading clerics of Shia Islam).

When I returned to Washington in 1973 after assignment to the Vietnam War, Iran dominated the nation's capital. The post-Vietnam workings of the Nixon Doctrine had made Iran into one of the world's "pivotal states" into which vast amounts of defense assistance were flowing. Iran, Kissinger said, provided a "geostrategic land bridge between Asia and Europe" and a bulwark against Soviet southward pressures. The Washington party scene was dominated by the extravagant wealth and charm of Iranian Ambassador Ardeshir Zahedi and a panoply of rich Iranian diplomats and deal-makers. From my new office in the State Department, I watched as Iranian students, silent with paper bags over their heads, daily passed almost endlessly around the building bearing "Down with the Shah!" signs. "Who are they?" I asked. "Why are they doing that?" The answer: "It's nothing, forget it."

By 1978, forces of revolution pressed heavily on the shah's regime as religiously fervent Islamists shoved other protest movements aside. The preeminent Parisian philosopher Michel Foucault went to Tehran in what would be a symbolically significant "intervention" by a paragon of the West's intelligentsia. Foucault adored what he called "the first great revolution against the global system." Although Foucault in the past had scorned Rousseau for having inspired much of the modern age's "governmentality," he described the Iranian Revolution in terms that perfectly expressed the anti-international-system prescriptions of Rousseau and Marx. This Islamist revolution would be not just political but total, transforming human nature itself because Islam "is not simply a religion but an entire way of life" with the potential to become "a gigantic powder keg, at the level of hundreds of millions of men." The Islamists also expressed "the perfectly unified collective will of the people," fulfilling Rousseau's definition of "The General Will." And, concluded Foucault, an Iranian Revolution could lead to a final dismantling of the sovereign state and an end to the Westphalian-Enlightenment design for a secular international order of state-to-state relations. The world, Foucault insisted, "must reject the thousand-year old portrayal of Muslims as fanatics."

THE INDIAN MUTINY AND THE INTERNATIONAL SYSTEM

Ranged across the turbulent modern centuries, the history of India displays powerful political, cultural, and religious oscillations of central importance to world affairs today.

In 1526 the Turko-Mongol warrior chief Babur began his conquest of India where, as emperor, he would found the Mughal Dynasty. Under Akbar the Great (reigned 1556–1605), Jahangir (1605–1627), and Aurangzeb (1658–1707), the Mughal court became the most sophisticated, learned, and artistically fabulous society in the world. Its Islamic character was lightly worn and most un-jihadist. The Taj Mahal, completed in 1640, remains the symbol of Mughal splendor.

In 1600 Queen Elizabeth chartered the East India Company as a monopoly for England's trade with the Eastern Hemisphere; by the late 1600s "John Company" was concentrating on India and rapidly gaining wealth and power. When Aurangzeb's exquisitely balanced political strategy was challenged by local revolts, the emperor began to impose a strict Islamic orthodoxy on India's non-Muslim peoples. As the Mughal realm fragmented, the company concluded political and economic agreements of mutual support with local potentates, enabling the English to play one ruler off another. A swift and vicious Persian foray ravaged Delhi in 1739 and left the Mughal dynasty a hollow shell. Robert Clive's victory over the French at Plassey in Bengal in 1757 made "the Honourable Company" the dominant de facto power in India. The Battle of Plassey was part of the Seven Years' War—in North America the French and Indian War—history's first truly *world* war.

As the company's successes expanded, Parliament in London sought control over such a profitable endeavor and in 1774 appointed Warren Hastings "Governor-General of British India." From this point forward India was at least nominally ruled from London. Although the company was relegated to an administrative role, the British in India kept London less than fully informed as the manly, plunging, enterprising first generations were succeeded by "men on stilts," Britons of a stature unequal to the task of disciplined governing; greed, sloth, and racism followed. Missionaries arrived from England to evangelize Hindus and Muslims alike, oblivious to the resentment they were stirring.

Lord Canning had foreseen what was coming. "In the sky of India," he had said, when taking up his post as governor-general, "a small cloud may rise, at first no bigger than a man's hand but which . . . may at last threaten to overwhelm us with ruin." Nonetheless, it was a shock when in 1857 came the world-historical upheaval of the Indian Mutiny, the rebellion of sepoys (native infantrymen) against their British officers and families. The causes were many and deep: the blatant exertion of British power over local rulers; harsh land reform measures; and insulting cultural practices. But the most inflammatory causes involved religion. If one religious affront would not summon the storm, another one would be found.

First came a new British army regulation subjecting Indian troops to overseas deployment to Burma; crossing the waters would mean a loss of caste. Then the issuance of ammunition for the new Enfield rifle inspired rumors that the cartridges were lubricated with animal fat from cows and pigs—horrifying for different reasons to Muslim and Hindu troopers alike. The uprising was hideous in its violence, and the reprisals merciless as the great rebellion was put down.

Profound consequences followed. The East India Company was abolished as Britain took direct rule; here was the start of the British Empire. Queen Victoria would be proclaimed Empress of India in 1877. Geopolitics on a world scale would be transformed as European powers maneuvered for control of the sea routes to the subcontinent and for influence on the Eurasian landmass in "The Great Game." Tactical after-effects would be felt in the disciplines of intelligence gathering and analysis, and new recognition of what would later be called "insurgency" and "counter-insurgency." Coming at a time when nationalism was emerging as a major factor in world politics, and revolutionary flames were fanned, the Indian Mutiny marked the first stirrings of "the Indian war of independence."

The most far-reaching influence generated by the mutiny was religious. Muslim sentiment had been smashed; the first reaction was to turn inward, to take a quietist approach, to seek refuge in doctrinal purity. The madrasa at Deoband would be a center for this. Over time this theologically intense movement would heighten anti-British and pan-Islamic feelings. The Deobandi movement would be seen in the late years of the next century as a progenitor of the Taliban. For their part, the British saw the need to build a new sense of Muslim identity and subsidized the Muhammadan Anglo-Oriental College at Aligarh, southeast of Delhi, where cricket would be played and Cambridge taken as a model with academic gowns worn as at Christ's College. Revealingly, Aligarh proposed cooperation with Deoband, but the latter would have none of it because the M.O.A. accepted Shia Muslims.

For Hindus, the process of consolidating a fragmented identity would take a slower course, yet emerge as *Hindutva*—Hinduness—and, in the person of Mahatma Gandhi and his call for *Hind Swaraj*, Indian self-rule. This would build pressure toward ending the British Raj even as it allowed Indian Muslims, led by Muhammed Ali Jinnah, to reach the conviction that only a separate Islamic state would enable Muslims to practice the faith fully. A reciprocal process of nationalism and religionism was launched.

All the forces came together in 1947 in what Winston Churchill would condemn as Britain's "shameful flight" from India and the catastrophic partition of British India, the jewel of the empire, into two sovereign states in the international system, with neither one psychologically, historically, culturally, or politically prepared for it. The circumstances of partition vastly favored India and left Pakistan democratically disabled, politically unstable, and unable to control the rise of Islamism.

Thus the record of British India from Plassy to partition is a story of modern world order in the making and in the maelstrom. All forms and dimensions are revealed, from the pre-modern empire to modern colonialism, imperialism, revolution, state-formation, war, and the return of religion to the Westphalian system which had sought to shelve it.

The international state system is a procedural structure. The substance of civic virtue that fills the structure is all-important. The legacy of the empire "on which the sun never set" would influence the course of world order long after what Kipling called its recessional, perhaps most stirringly declared in the dedication by the Bengali scholar-intellectual Nirad Chaudhuri to his *Autobiography of an Unknown Indian*, 1951:

To the Memory of the
British Empire in India
Which Conferred Subjecthood on US
But Withheld Citizenship;
To Which Yet
Every One of US Threw Out the Challenge
"Civis Britannicus Sum"
Because
All that was Good and Living

Within Us
Was Made, Shaped, and Quickened
By the Same British Rule

Britain's empire spread the forms of the Westphalian system around the world and invested them with substantive ideals of open trade, open expression, and popular sovereignty that would define the major aspirations for world order in the twentieth century.

CHAPTER FOUR

An Islamist Challenge Takes Shape

NOT UNTIL THE OPENING of the twenty-first century did American leaders begin to comprehend the sources, extent, and objectives of Islamism's rise through the later decades of the twentieth century. In retrospect, 1979 was a turning point.

1979: IRAN

The most significant turning point of 1979 was the Iranian Revolution led by the Ayatollah Khomeini, a world-historical event possessing the ideological potential of the French Revolution of 1789 and the Russian Revolution of 1917—each one a fundamental challenge to the established international order. The Iranian Revolution brought to power for the first time in history an Islamist regime in full control of a state within the international state system and with a theologically grounded agenda which rejected every core principle of international order. And in gaining power, the ayatollah's revolution had over-thrown one of the most prominent, wealthy, and militarily power-ful of America's allies, a linchpin of "The Nixon Doctrine": the imperial kingdom of Mohammad Reza Shah Pahlavi. This was no ordinary revolution.

Consciously or not, the ayatollah's governmental structure was designed in accord with that described in Jean-Jacques Rousseau's *Social Contract*, a manual for the revolutionary overthrow of all established governance and the creation of the world's first ever "legitimate" society. Such revolutionary regimes relegate governmental ministries and the military to politically marginal roles. Above them are the ideologically empowered keepers of "the will of the people," which operate as duplicative, more potent versions of institutions below them (as the Iranian Revolutionary Guard Command does vis-à-vis the army). And at the very top is a single all-powerful figure who both transcends and permeates the entire society, a Great Helmsman, Maximum Leader, Dear Leader, or Supreme Guide.

To gain this preeminent revolutionary status, Khomeini invented a new political philosophy for Shia Islam during his 1964–78 exile. In place of the doctrine that clerics should refrain from activism in government pending the reappearance of the hidden Twelfth Imam (the Mahdi in occultation), Khomeini promulgated the *Velayat-e Faqih*, the "Rule of the Jurists," which would legitimate a theocratic regime for Iran under a single supreme figure, the ayatollah himself.

Of the two "Rousseau-esque" levels of the Iranian polity, the greater theocratic level of power and the lesser one administer-ing governmental agencies, only the latter would be allowed a semblance of democratic elections. The real power of the Islamic Republic was theologically legitimated, above and beyond the reach of voters.

The vivid marker of revolutionary Iran's opposition to international order would be its 1979 seizure of the American embassy and hostage-taking in violation of the first principle of the Westphalian international system, diplomatic immunity. Then followed its secret drive to acquire nuclear weapons in violation of international law and its support for terrorist operations beyond its borders, all conducted under a rhetoric aimed at bridging the Sunni-Shia divide as a way to make Iran the sole hegemonic power over the entire region and all Islam beyond.

Kissinger, writing in 1979 just after the shah had been overthrown and had fled to the United States and then Egypt, noted in sorrow that the shah's Iran had been "one of America's best, most important, and most loyal friends in the world." At the same time, Foreign Service Officer Henry Precht, the desk officer for Iran, spoke to a jampacked auditorium at the State Department to assure the Foreign Service that the United States certainly could "do business" with the new regime. The Imperial Kingdom of Iran now would be the Islamic Republic of Iran. Neither ever had been nor would be a true member of the international state system.

1979: SAUDI ARABIA

In 1979 the Grand Mosque in Mecca was seized by a fanatical Islamist group led by a charismatic figure representing a more

primitively authentic version of the faith than that promulgated by the Saudi regime. Saudi authorities, with the hushed-
up help of French commandos, brutally put down the uprising,
but the incident induced the regime in effect to adopt the
extreme agenda of the leader of the attack. The Saudi rulers
sought to control the Islamists by imposing even more rigid
religious strictures on the population and by providing abundant
resources to subsidize Wahabi-Salafi Islamism in other countries around the region and the world. Incited by claims that
the mosque seizure had been instigated by the United States,
anti-American demonstrations took place in several Muslim
countries and the American embassy in Islamabad was burned
to the ground.

1979: PAKISTAN

The year 1979 also marked a major turn in Pakistan when
President Zia ul-Haq ordered the judicial murder of Prime Minister Zulfikar Ali Bhutto and began to stake his regime's legitimacy and political survival on bringing Islamist factions into
some key functions of government. By this decision, Pakistan
abandoned the secular state vision of founding father Muhammad Ali Jinnah. From 1979 on, every Pakistan government
would be gravely strained by its need to both use and yet control its Islamist partners, and Islamist infiltration of supposedly
off-limits governmental security agencies could not be halted.
Pakistan's leaders began to employ Islamist terrorists to challenge
India in Kashmir and to gain strategic influence in Afghanistan.

What seemed at first to be a brilliant policy would eventually threaten Pakistan's survival as a state.

1979: AFGHANISTAN

In 1979, the Soviet Union seized Afghanistan, installed a puppet military regime, and declared it the "Democratic Republic of Afghanistan." This, one of the last acts of open warfare of the cold war, transmogrified in the years following into a signal propaganda victory for Islamists and their global cause. Military weaponry and training support given by Pakistan and the United States to Afghan tribesmen as "Freedom Fighters" against the Soviet army would bring victory to the Mujahidin, who would arouse Islamists all across the Muslim world and be seen as progenitors of the Taliban and al-Qaeda. The latter's leader, Osama bin Laden, would claim that the Mujahidin had defeated the stronger of Islam's global adversaries, the Soviet Union, so Islamists now could confidently take on the weaker one, the United States.

1979: EGYPT

In 1979, President Anwar Sadat became the first Arab leader to make peace with Israel, causing Egypt to be deposed as the leader of the Arab world and Sadat to be assassinated by Islamists two years later. Egypt's expulsion by the Arab League would be seized by Saddam Hussein as an opportunity to push his Iraqi regime to the forefront of the Arab world through anti-Israel, anti-U.S., and anti-U.N. actions.

1979: Saddam's Iraq—Bonfire of the Pathologies

On National Day, July 17, 1979, Saddam Hussein declared himself president of Iraq, placing his predecessor under house arrest. Saddam then conducted his own version of "The Terror" of the French Revolution in a bloody purge of the Ba'ath Party. As Professor Bernard Lewis pointed out, Saddam's dictatorship presided over a political party that was an amalgam of the Nazi and Communist parties as viewed from the Middle East in the mid-twentieth century.

Saddam then proceeded to employ Iraq's national powers as a constant menace to his neighbors in the region and as an ever-worsening adversary of the international system, soon becoming the major continuing preoccupation of the United Nations Security Council through his challenges to the maintenance of "international peace and security" as set forth in the U.N. Charter.

The case of Saddam Hussein's dictatorship is of immense significance. He perfected a strategy of having it both ways. On the one hand, he shielded his actions behind the privileges and immunities of the international system, such as non-intervention into the internal affairs of a sovereign state. On the other hand, he used the powers of the Iraqi state to violate the laws and principles of the international system in multiple ways. For years, the leading nations of the world let him get away with it.

After fourteen months of consolidating his power, Saddam on September 22, 1980, ordered his army to invade Iran, to weaken the ayatollah's revolutionary attraction to Iraq's Shia population. Thus was launched an almost decade-long war whose mutual slaughter would be compared to World War I's trench warfare. In response, the United States pursued a strategy later called "dual containment" aimed at exhausting both sides while trying to contain the war from spreading to the rest of the region. In 1987 the fighting began to threaten shipping in the Persian Gulf to the point where the Gulf Arab states requested American naval protection. When oil tankers were "re-flagged" under American registry, the U.S. Navy escorted them up and down the Gulf. The reflagging operation was a diplomatic triumph supported by the first-ever 15–0 U.N. Security Council resolution, setting the stage for the United Nations to oversee an end to the Iran-Iraq War in 1988.

Two years later Saddam ordered his armed forces to invade Kuwait. He committed war crimes. He took hostages. He launched ballistic missiles against a third and then a fourth country in the region.

The Kuwait war was unique in modern times because Saddam had totally eradicated a legitimate state of the international system and turned it into "Province 19" of Iraq. Aggressors in wars typically seize some territory or occupy the defeated country in order to install a puppet regime. Saddam erased Kuwait from the map of the world.

That got the world's attention. That's why at the United Nations the votes were wholly in favor of a U.S.-led military operation—Desert Storm—to throw Saddam out of Kuwait and

restore Kuwait to its place as a legitimate state in the international system. There was virtually universal recognition that
those responsible for the international system of states could
not let one of its member states simply be rubbed out.

Saddam's aggression was illuminated by two symbolic acts of
Islamist significance. King Hussein of Jordan, Sandhurst edu-
cated and welcomed by the West as a sound and sympathetic
statesman, suddenly declared his support for Saddam's war and,
separately, declared his claim to the title of Sharif of Mecca
once held by his great-grandfather. Saddam Hussein then added
Takbir—meaning the phrase *Allahu Akbar*—in his hand's own
script to Iraq's national flag. A monarch and a military dictator
were announcing their submission to a new Islamist order sub-
suming the sovereign state.

When the American-led coalition forces drove Saddam's
army back into Iraq, President Bush could not order the
U.S. Army to drive on to Baghdad to overthrow Saddam's dictatorship because the diplomacy which built the coalition had
been predicated on agreement to liberate Kuwait, nothing more.

So in 1991 a cease-fire was put in place. Then the U.N.
Security Council decided that, in order to prevent Saddam
from starting more wars or committing further crimes against
his own people, he must give up his arsenal of weapons of mass
destruction.

Here is how it was supposed to work. If Saddam cooperated
with U.N. inspectors, produced his weapons, and facilitated
their destruction, then the cease-fire would be transformed into
a peace agreement, ending the state of war between the inter-

national system and Iraq. But if Saddam did *not* cooperate, and materially breached his obligations regarding his weapons of mass destruction, then the original U.N. Security Council authorization for the use of "all necessary force" against Iraq— an authorization suspended but not canceled at the end of Desert Storm—would be reactivated and Saddam would face another round of U.S.-led military action. Saddam agreed to this arrangement.

In the early 1990s, U.N. inspectors found plenty of material in the category of weapons of mass destruction and dismantled a lot of it. They kept on finding such weapons, but as the pressure of force declined, Saddam's cooperation declined. He began to play games to obstruct and undermine the inspection effort.

By 1998, the situation had become untenable. Saddam had made inspections impossible. President Clinton in February 1998 declared that Saddam would have to comply with the U.N. resolutions or face American military force. U.N. Secretary-General Kofi Annan flew to Baghdad and returned with a new promise of cooperation from Saddam. But Saddam did not cooperate. The U.S. Congress then passed the Iraq Liberation Act by a vote of 360 to 38 in the House of Representatives; the Senate gave its unanimous consent. Signed into law on October 31, 1998, H.R. 4655 supported the renewed use of force against Saddam with the objective of changing the regime. By this time, Saddam had openly rejected the inspections and all the U.N. resolutions.

In November 1998, the Security Council passed Resolution 1205 declaring Saddam to be in flagrant violation of all

U.N. resolutions going back to 1991. This terminated the cease-fire and reactivated the original authorization for the use of force against Saddam. President Clinton ordered American forces into action in December 1998 in an operation called "Desert Fox."

But the U.S. called off its military operation after only four days—at first stating respect for Ramadan, then apparently because President Clinton did not feel able to lead the country into war at a time when he was facing impeachment.

So inspections stopped. The United States ceased to take the lead. But the inspectors reported that, as of the end of 1998, Saddam possessed major quantities of weapons of mass destruction across a range of categories, particularly in chemical and biological weapons, and the means of delivering them by missiles. The intelligence services of the world agreed. In *The New Republic* of December 21, 1998, former inspector Scott Ritter wrote that Saddam's Iraq as of then had:

- Its entire nuclear weapons infrastructure intact
- Components for up to four nuclear devices and the ability to produce a highly enriched uranium fissile core
- Long-range ballistic missiles and mobile launchers
- An extensive covert procurement network for prohibited capabilities
- Anthrax, botulinum toxin, and clostridium perfringens to fill bombs and missile warheads
- Tons of VX nerve gas and mustard gas
- The infrastructure and "cookbooks" to reconstitute large-scale chemical and nuclear weapons quickly.

Saddam was left undisturbed to do as he wished with this arsenal of weapons and to rule Iraq as a rogue state. The international system had given up its responsibility to monitor and deal with this major threat.

THE LOST DECADE OF THE 1990S

All through the 1990s Saddam Hussein's Iraq had been an omnidirectional adversary of the international system. The larger context of international security, after a positive start, had turned negative as well. After the fall of communism, democratic states and the international community turned to the work of rebuilding, for the cold war had damaged them both. As the 1990s began, countries in every part of the world sought to move toward democracy, and the United States and the United Nations began to respond to their requests for help.

The post-cold-war decade of the 1990s, which might have been expected to usher in an overhaul of the international system of states and its restoration to something like its former status, instead brought further deterioration. President George H.W. Bush took the problem seriously, speaking about a "new world order" and gently suggesting, in a speech to the United Nations General Assembly in September 1991, that a *pax universalis* somehow might be built on the "coalition model" followed by those who fought to drive Saddam Hussein's forces out of Kuwait. The United Nations seemed to gain new respectability with the first-ever summit of heads of state and government, which met at the Security Council on January 31, 1992, and

authorized Secretary-General Boutros Boutros-Ghali to find
ways through which the United Nations might live up to the
original vision of its 1945 Charter.

But the international system continued to suffer damage
and deterioration during the 1990s. Bill Clinton's presidential
victory in 1992, taken as a mandate from a cold-war-weary
electorate to turn attention to the domestic agenda, ended
any sustained effort by the United States to repair and renew
the foundations of world order. This broke what had been a
pattern in modern history. After every major war of the past
three centuries or so, the victors came together to try to refurbish, reconstruct, and repair the international system. First in
the series was the Treaty of Westphalia that concluded the
Thirty Years' War in 1648. The 1815 Congress of Vienna,
the 1919 Treaty of Versailles, and the 1945 United Nations
Charter followed this pattern. But the post-cold-war period
produced no similar international attempt to shore up and
refurbish the international state system.

Worse still, the state itself—the building block of the
structure—suffered devastating setbacks, as the realization
emerged that a sovereign, independent U.N. member state
could fail, and its legitimate government could disappear. This
happened in Somalia, where the United Nations attempted
to deal with the situation by launching something new—a
"humanitarian intervention." This initiative failed when the
country leading the effort, the United States, pulled back out
after the "Black Hawk Down" disaster in Mogadishu in 1993.
Then the state in Afghanistan failed, and states elsewhere in

Asia, Africa, and Latin America began to lose control of sub-
stantial areas of their hinterlands.

The United Nations itself, as "The World Organization,"
was hit hard during the 1990s. Along with the collapse of the
state in Somalia, and the United Nations' humanitarian effort
there, came ethnic cleansing in Bosnia, genocide in Rwanda,
and crimes against humanity in Sierra Leone. In every case,
decisions by the member states of the U.N. Security Council
humiliated and discredited that body's proudest attribute—its
peacekeeping function—either by providing no action when
action was called for or by putting defenseless peacekeepers into
a raging war where there was no peace to keep. In 1995, after
the United States and NATO finally acted to stop the slaughter
in Bosnia, they deliberately excluded the United Nations from
the Dayton peace negotiations. Then in 1999 they launched an
air war for Kosovo without making the slightest effort to gain
U.N. Security Council authorization.

During the post-cold-war decade, international law was weakened from the inside by the zeal of its most devoted adherents.
The assaults took place on two levels. First was the series of
international peace agreements that were poorly executed from
a diplomatic negotiator's point of view: unbalanced (Oslo),
politically unrealistic (Kyoto), out of date (START II), con-
ceptually incoherent (Dayton), or avoiding the toughest issues
(Irish Agreement).

Second, and more deleterious over the longer term, was the
drive to negotiate into permanent existence international institutions that in large part would be untethered to the states that

signed on to them. Prominent in this category was the Ottawa process, which led to an anti-land mine treaty brought about by a coalition of nongovernmental organizations and states, led by Canada, none of whom bore the major burden of maintaining international peace and security. The treaty came into force without the support of states representing more than half the world's population and without regard for the military necessity of land mines to deter renewed warfare across, for example, the DMZ between North and South Korea.

A similar coalition of activists, lawyers, bureaucrats, and an umbrella nongovernmental organization, the Coalition for the International Criminal Court (ICC), pushed through the Rome Statute, which created the ICC through a concoction of novel procedures that bypassed ways of deliberating and deciding considered essential for legitimacy within the international system of states. The result was a new global institution with legal definitions that under American law would be considered "void for vagueness" and a prosecutor whose powers ranged well beyond the reach of a sovereign state.

Even more than politicians, intellectuals and academics undermined the international system. They declared that sovereignty was "organized hypocrisy" and that the state was outmoded or that the powers of government should be devolved to lower levels or be given up to new forms of authority floating high above the state. For a time it appeared that with the achievement of the European Union, the Westphalian international system of states, born on the Continent three and a half centuries before, might be on its way out. As this intellectual and administrative farewell to the international system of states in Europe was emerging, the international system of states for the world at large was deteriorating, the victim of neglect, ignorance, and indifference.

THE ISLAMIST WAR ON WORLD ORDER, WELL UNDER WAY

The Economist of August 6, 1994, ran a special "Survey of Islam." The cover depicted Christian knights and mounted Muslim warriors—led by Richard the Lionheart and Saladin—in battle, with the headline: "Not Again, for Heaven's Sake," an archetypical image of the two opposing religion-civilizations in irrepressible confrontation.

We can trace the roots of the twentieth-century phase of the confrontation at least as far back as 1914 when, as we have seen, the Ottoman Empire chose to enter the Great War on the side of Imperial Germany. The kaiser's Germany and its Ottoman partner lost, the Ottoman Empire collapsed, and when in 1924 the caliphate—the sole form of overall governance of the Islamic world—was abolished, a process was set in place that would establish states all across the Arab-Islamic Middle East; none would be democratic.

In the years that followed, the Arab states would remain impervious to worldwide trends toward government by consent of the governed as region after region was swept by a wave of democratization, including:

- After World War II, when Germany and Japan, under American tutelage, turned decisively toward democracy
- In the mid-century era of de-colonization, which saw India become the world's largest democracy
- In the post-cold war period, when countries in every part of the world sought open political and economic systems, and the United Nations for the first time responded by helping set up elections and democratic political institutions.

Through all these changes, the Arab Middle East resolutely remained the one region without a single democratic government. Looking back on these decades, the Arab Human Development Report of 2002—an "unbiased, objective analysis" by "a group of distinguished Arab intellectuals," as the U.N.-published document stated—found that the region was uniquely impaired by its own bad governance. For generations, the report found, people of the Arab world have been hindered from acquiring information and have been denied freedom of expression. Beyond that, Arab governments have suppressed the intellectual and social capabilities of half the population—Arab women. The Report put it starkly: "The wave of democracy that transformed governance in most of Latin America and East Asia in the 1980s and Eastern Europe and much of Central Asia in the late 1980s and early 1990s has barely reached the Arab states. This freedom deficit undermines human development and is one of the most painful manifestations of lagging political development. . . . Fate has not decreed that political power in the Arab world should permanently exclude participation by citizens."

The varieties of Arab misrule over the decades since the end of the First World War produced economic, social, and political pathologies that provided fertile ground for the steady growth of a revolutionary religious ideology bent on taking command of the Middle East and turning the region as a whole against the rest of the world.

What might be called the First Terrorist War was fought in the 1970s and 1980s: Israeli Olympic athletes murdered; a Palestinian attempt to overthrow the government of Jordan; passengers gunned down at airline ticket counters; American embassy personnel taken hostage; the hijacking of TWA Flight 847 and the cruise ship *Achille Lauro*; the bombing of a Berlin discotheque.

In the 1980s, Secretary of State George Shultz tried to convince congressmen and media commentators that the slogan "one man's terrorist is another man's freedom fighter" was false and dangerous. The Reagan administration focused on how to defend against terrorism by reinforcing our embassies and increasing intelligence efforts. We thought we made some progress. A legal basis was established for holding states responsible for supporting or harboring terrorists, or directing terrorist acts. Through intelligence, many planned terrorist acts were blocked, but American administrations really did not understand what motivated the terrorists or what they were out to do.

For years, American administrations failed to recognize Islamism's role in terrorism because foreign affairs specialists assumed such acts must be politically motivated. The Westphalian credo had done its work: religion was out of the question when it came to international diplomacy. The Foreign Service had been profoundly affected when in 1973 the American ambassador and the deputy chief of mission in Khartoum were seized at a diplomatic reception and murdered the next day. The killers came from the Palestinian group Black September acting, it was said, on orders from Palestinian Liberation Organization Chairman Yasser Arafat. To the American diplomatic establishment, the PLO was an indispensable interlocutor in "the peace process" and its stated political objective was a "secular democratic bi-national state"—nothing religious about it. When Egypt's Sadat was assassinated in 1981, American officials were simply blind to the fact that the perpetrators were Islamists; not until the 1990s, when the 1981 videos were reviewed, would the obvious Islamist role be recognized.

Saddam Overthrown

President Bush made it clear by 2002 that Saddam must be brought into compliance with the long string of U.N. Chapter VII resolutions. Obviously, the international system could not leave this situation as it was. The United States decided to continue to work within the scope of the U.N. Security Council resolutions—all seventeen of them, dating back to 1991—to deal with Saddam.

In late 2002, after an excruciating American diplomatic effort, the Security Council passed Resolution 1441, which gave Saddam one final chance to comply or face military force. On December 8, 2002, Iraq produced its required report. Thousands of pages long, the report did not in any way account for the remaining weapons of mass destruction (WMD) that the U.N.

inspectors had reported to be in existence at the end of 1998. Chief U.N. inspector Hans Blix stated to the Security Council on January 27, 2003, that Iraq had not complied with Resolution 687 of 1991 or subsequent resolutions, that Iraq had not come to a genuine acceptance "of the disarmament which was demanded of it."

That should have been that. But the debate at the United Nations went on and on. The Bush administration then attempted to show its U.N. audience evidence that Saddam possessed weapons of mass destruction, an effort that only distorted the true international legal case for military action. Instead of focusing on Iraq and Saddam, France induced others to regard the problem as one of restraining the United States—a position that seemed to emerge from France's aspirations for greater influence in the European Union. By March 2003, it was clear that French diplomacy had split NATO, the European Union, and the U.N. Security Council and probably had convinced Saddam that he would never face the use of force. The French position, in effect, was that Saddam was beginning to show signs of cooperation with the U.N. resolutions because more than 200,000 American troops were poised on Iraq's borders, ready to strike. Thus the United States should just keep its troops poised there until presumably France would instruct the Americans to withdraw or go into action. This, of course, was impossible militarily, politically, and financially.

Beyond power politics lay a firm foundation for American action. Key points need to be emphasized:

- There had never been a clearer case of an outlaw state using its privileges of statehood to advance its dictator's

interests in ways that defied and endangered the international state system.

- The international legal case against Saddam—seventeen
  resolutions—was unprecedented.

- The intelligence services of all involved nations and
  the U.N. inspectors during more than a decade agreed
  that Saddam possessed weapons of mass destruction that
  posed a threat to international peace and security.

- Saddam had four undisturbed years to augment, con-
  ceal, or disperse his arsenal.

- The Duelfer Report, accepted as "the final word" on
  Saddam's weapons program, declared (in 2004) that "as
  U.N. sanctions eroded there was a concomitant expansion of activities that could support full WMD reactiva-
  tion . . . Over time, sanctions had steadily weakened to
  the point where Iraq, in 2000–2001, was confidently
  designing missiles around components that could only
  be obtained outside sanctions. . . . Baghdad exploited
  the mechanism for executing the Oil-for-Food program
  to give individuals and countries an economic stake in
  ending sanctions."

- Saddam used every means to avoid cooperating or
  explaining what he had done with the weapons. His
  refusal in itself was, under the U.N. resolutions, adequate
  grounds for resuming the military operation against him
  that had been put in abeyance in 1991.

- President Bush stated that he was ordering U.S. forces
  into action under U.N. Security Council Resolutions 678
  and 687, the bases for military action against Saddam

Hussein in 1991. Those who criticize the United States for unilateralism should recognize that no nation in the history of the United Nations has ever engaged in such a sustained multilateral diplomatic effort to adhere to the principles of international law and organization within the international system. In the end, it was the United States that upheld and acted in accordance with the U.N. resolutions on Iraq, not those on the Security Council who tried to stop it.

• In the months after the fall of Saddam Hussein, the U.N. Security Council unanimously passed three resolutions in support of American policy: 1483, authorizing the United States and Britain as the legal occupying powers in Iraq; 1511, recognizing the Iraqi Governing Council; and 1546, authorizing the interim Iraqi government and setting out a detailed timetable for direct elections facilitated by the United Nations. For the first time, the U.N. Security Council came down unambiguously for democratization in the Middle East.

Saddam's Strategy

The mystery of what Saddam Hussein was up to has become clearer over time.

In mid-1991, Saddam faced the classic Arab dilemma: he had just lost a war but had to depict it as a great victory to his people and the Arab world. He had done this before. He had big decisions to make regarding his weapons of mass destruction, which were both a program and an on-the-ground inventory. The arguments cut both ways, with the pros and cons almost equal. On the one hand, he faced U.N. sanctions and the threat that if he did not disarm the war could be resumed, this time inside Iraq, not in Kuwait. That argued for giving up his stocks of WMD, as did the probability that inspectors would find and destroy them anyway. Or he could eliminate the physical WMD but keep the program as a "virtual" WMD capability, ready to resume production when the heat was off.

On the other hand, there was Saddam's documented conviction that WMD are of inestimable value, a wholly desirable category of goods. Saddam needed them to deter Iran from another Iran-Iraq war. Perhaps more important was the fearsome prestige that possession of WMDs conferred upon Saddam when it came to intimidating his military commanders, the Iraqi people (especially the Kurds and Shia), and his Arab neighbors. If the Americans believed Saddam possessed WMD it would be a deterrent against their taking military action against him.

So in the first phase of his strategy, Saddam Hussein played it both ways. He cooperated with the U.N. inspectors, who found plenty of WMD and dismantled them; this gave Saddam leverage on the lifting of sanctions. But then he reversed direction, no longer cooperating with but impeding the work of the inspectors. He began to claim to the United Nations that he no longer had WMD, even as he signaled to the Arab world that he indeed did possess such weapons and that he was upholding Arab pride by defying the pressures of the infidels. And quietly he was maintaining his virtual programs in readiness for a more propitious time.

The second phase came as a godsend to Saddam. As an aide to U.N. Secretary-General Boutros Boutros-Ghali, I was a close-in but guileless participant in it. In the mid-1990s pressures grew in Europe and the United States against the sanctions, which were hurting the Iraqi people, not Saddam. When American ambassador to the United Nations Madeleine Albright came to speak at Yale Law School, demonstrators disrupted her speech with incessant shouts of "baby killer."

In this environment, the "Oil-for-Food" U.N. Program was undertaken. Boutros-Ghali took the lead in setting up the mechanism, with U.N. legal counsel Hans Corell as the chief negotiator. The negotiations with Saddam's top henchmen were convoluted and perplexing, as set forth in revealing detail in Boutros-Ghali's memoir *Unvanquished*. We could not understand why this effort, which after all was humanitarian and at least a partial easing of the sanctions (which Saddam Hussein had always sought), could be so maddeningly difficult to achieve. Suddenly came a flash of insight: Saddam was manipulating the headlines—"Negotiations on Track" one day; "Negotiations Broken Off" the next—to play the oil market. He held the media's on-off switch in his hand and so knew in advance whether the price would rise or fall. At the end, the United Nations did reach an agreement with Saddam's Iraq. But it was a weak one, accepted out of frustration with the Iraqi negotiators and under continuing pressure from the Europeans and the American liberal establishment to "do something—anything" to relieve the suffering of the Iraqi people. When Albright protested that the agreement was one that "you could drive a truck through," she was understating it.

The Oil-for-Food Program was the answer to Saddam's prayers. He could manipulate it to reduce (selectively) the effect of the sanctions on the people, to get kickbacks, to bribe European companies and officials, to rake in billions to build palaces and buy weapons abroad. (The *New York Times* page 1 article on the Duelfer Report was headlined, "US Report Says Saddam Bought Arms With Ease.") And the oil contracts and payoffs to Europeans and to U.N. officials would mean that they could be counted on to oppose any American military action against him.

The third phase was also a kind of inside-out gift to Saddam. His "gaming" of the inspections had been succeeding wonderfully. On several occasions his violations of U.N. resolutions had led the Clinton administration to mobilize for action, at times ordering carrier task forces and other military assets to steam toward the Gulf. Every time, however, Saddam at the critical moment would declare a willingness to "negotiate" and the United States would turn back. Joy—and laughter—then must have been unconfined in Saddam's palace operations room.

Saddam's strategy had worked. Some of the sanctions had been eased, and international pressure to do more in that direction continued. The inspectors were gone with no sign of returning. Saddam was growing Croesus-like from the Oil-for-Food billions. He was buying conventional weapons with ease despite the sanctions. The United States had taken its best shots at him, but it had been rebuffed or had retreated at every turn. His generals, the Iraqi people, the Iranians, the Arab world, and the world at large feared his arsenal of WMD. At that point, Saddam had become the central potentate of the Middle East in every sense of that word. And he had adopted an Islamist persona.

United Nations Security Council Resolution 1441 of late 2002 was not necessary; enough international legal authority for military action against Saddam was already in place. But Resolution 1441 was good to have for "Operation Iraqi Freedom," which President Bush launched in March 2003. Saddam surely thought that enough European and U.N. officials had been bought off or cowed to ensure that Bush could never pull off the diplomatic success and coalition-building his father had achieved in 1990–91. But Saddam had miscalculated then, and he miscalculated again in 2003.

The most important aspect of the Iraq War has been what it meant for the integrity of the international system and for the effort to deal effectively with terrorism. The stakes were huge, and the terrorists knew it, which explained their tactics in Iraq. And that is why, for us and for our allies, failure was not an option. The United States and others who recognize the need to sustain the international system must no longer acquiesce in the takeover of states by dictators who carry on their depredations—including the development of awesome weapons for threats, use, or sale—behind the shield of protection that statehood provides. No criminal in charge of a state should be allowed to continue to demand the privileges and immunities of a system he seeks to destroy.

A respected expert on international affairs—one who was not supportive of President Bush (Thomas Powers in the *New York Review of Books*, March 11, 2004)—stated it dramatically: the "plan to transform the Islamic world beginning with Iraq . . .

represents what is possibly the single most ambitious program to change the world in American history. Not even the fabled Marshall Plan for rebuilding Europe after World War II matches it for imagination, generosity, sweep—and difficulty."

As our most profound thinker on the Arab and Middle Eastern world, Fouad Ajami, has pointed out, the terrorists of 9/11 "came out of the pathologies of Arab political life. Their financiers were Arabs and so were those crowds in Cairo and Nablus and Amman that had winked at the terror and had seen those attacks as America getting its comeuppance on that terrible day. Kabul had not sufficed as a return address in the twilight war; it was important to take the war into the Arab world itself, and the despot in Baghdad had drawn the short straw. He had been brazen and defiant at a time of genuine American concern, and a lesson was made of him . . . The ruler in Baghdad was a favored son of that Arab nation. The decapitation of his regime was a cautionary tale for his Arab brethren. Grant George W. Bush his due. He drew a line when the world of the Arabs was truly in the wind and played upon by powerful temptations."

CHAPTER FIVE

The Shock of Recognition

T
HE ATTACKS OF SEPTEMBER 11, 2001, were fortunate in one sense: they forced the United States to focus on the situation which led to them and on the dimensions of the challenge. In a sense, the world awakened to the threat at a relatively early stage. Had the 9/11 attacks been held off for some years, further deterioration in the established mechanisms of world order might have made its defense far more difficult, even impossible.

What we have been witnessing is nothing short of a civil war in the Arab-Islamic world. On one side are those regimes in the Arab-Islamic world that, after appeasing, trying to buy off, or propagandizing the terrorists, have begun to recognize that, as members of the international state system, they must find a way to reconcile their Islamic beliefs and practices with it. On the other side are those who, for Islamist ideological reasons, reject the international system of states, international law and organization, international values and principles, such as human rights, and the use of diplomacy to work through problems. The distinction between Islamic and Islamist is imperative.

Islamists follow a doctrine that cannot accept or participate in or with the international order:

- The state, as the basic unit of the international system, is by definition un-Islamic in that it fragments a people that should be one community (*Umma*). So for Muslims to be part of the state system opens them to the charge of apostasy—and in Islam there is nothing worse.
- The state, under the international system begun with the Treaty of Westphalia, must have a secular character in its international dealings. (The 1648 treaty fostered this understanding as a way to avoid further wars of religion.) Such a secular dimension is unacceptable to Islamists.
- International law similarly is unacceptable as it falls outside and in many ways could not accommodate *sharia*, to Islamists the only law governing Muslims.
- Similarly, democracy, which in the modern era increasingly has come to be part of the accepted international order, cannot be tolerated by Islamists, as it requires equal justice under laws made by representatives of the people. This would amount to an ongoing violation of *sharia*.
- International norms and agreements on human rights, such as the rights of women, do not accord with the Islamist interpretation of *sharia*.

In the largest context, an unbreakable logic chain imposes an insurmountable barrier between Islamism and the established international system. Islamists claim, first, that the originating source of the international system lies in the duality expressed at Christianity's founding: "Render unto Caesar that which is Caesar's; unto God that which is God's." This division of temporal and spiritual realms is what Islam brought to an end with the message of the Prophet.

Second, they claim that the modern international order is a secularized version of this Christian duality: the separation of church and state, of public and private, and of powers with "checks and balances." All are anathema to the unity and wholeness of Islam.

Therefore, any participation in the international order is impossible for Islamists to tolerate. As an example, Saudi Arabia, which bases its regime on the strictest fundamentalist reading of the Quran, is considered by Islamists to be un-Islamic and apostate simply because it is a state within the international state system.

Over the past two decades, four major phenomena have emerged in the Middle East and other Muslim areas, posing an interrelated set of threats to world order. First, governance in some states collapsed or lost control of parts of once-sovereign territory. This shocking and unanticipated development of international affairs called forth the then-new concept of "failed states." Second, it soon appeared that these ungoverned spaces of the world were becoming bases in which non-state, terror-using Islamist groups could recruit, arm, plan, and train for attacks on targets in and beyond the Muslim world.

The ideology and strategy of these groups—al-Qaeda most notably among them—called for attacks and subversive actions that would:

1. Bring an end to non-Muslim governmental and private sector presence in Islamic lands
2. End outside support for virtually all regimes now governing states in the Middle East
3. Take Islamist control of one or more such states
4. Move toward the establishment of a "sharia State" (some would say ultimately a caliphate) as the globe-spanning governing authority for all Islam
5. Move in parallel to extend a similar process for Europe, Central Asia, South and Southeast Asia, Africa, and the western hemisphere, wherever and whenever possible.

The third development was the realization that governing regimes of several Arab states had turned themselves into "enablers" of these enemies of international order. The pattern, set by Saudi Arabia, involved enhanced promulgation of radical instruction, subsidies for non-state terror-using groups, and incessant propagandizing of the population to instill a semi-conspiratorial, one-issue explanation narrative. What was this narrative? It was that all problems of the region and the faith stemmed from Israel's oppression of the Palestinians; that the United States bore a core responsibility in that its policies were uniformly pro-Israel, Washington being under the control of American Jews; and that nothing could be asked or expected of the Arab-Islamic world in any regard until the Palestine problem is solved—the solution generally being described as the de facto end of the State of Israel through the demographic means of a Palestinian "right of return."

The fourth phenomenon was the rise of "rogue" regimes, states that are recognized as legitimate members of the international state system and entitled to its privileges and immunities yet, at the same time, are ideologically committed adversaries of the international system. This dual role provides the "rogue" state with an on-off switch in its foreign policy: it can take a number of wrongful actions in pursuit of its own interest until, facing harsh countermeasures from the international community, it suddenly announces its readiness to negotiate or otherwise comply with normal international procedures—this in the sure knowledge that the outside world will welcome the rogue's "change of heart." Some typical headlines from articles in the *New York Times* of 2008 demonstrate this pattern:

a. "Softer Tone from Iran Has Experts Guessing"

b. "Iran Substantially Shifts Position, Makes Counter-Offer to 5 + 1 Package; Atmospherics are Changed"

c. "Ahmadinejad Says There Will Be No War With Israel or U.S."

d. "Iran Nuclear Negotiator to Meet in Geneva with EU Foreign Minister Next Weekend: US Under Secretary to Join Talks; First US-Iran Contact Since 1978"

e. "Geneva Talks Go Nowhere; Rice: 'Sick of Stalling'"

f. "Iran is Conduit for Jihadis Moving From Iraq to Afghan-Pakistan Fighting"

g. "Ahmadinejad at Durban II Conference in Geneva
   Threatens Israel"

Steps (a) through (d) are in the accommodating mode;
(e) through (g) are confrontational. We can anticipate that
(h) through (k) will be accommodationist again. All this
would be managed so as to manipulate the world oil market
for Iran's gain and to ensure that wrongdoing steps, i.e., those
that further Iran's agenda, will outweigh its cooperative
actions by about three to one.

Over the course of many years this tactic has worked again and
again as a means of neutralizing world pressure while going
forward with the regime's illicit activities. We have seen the
pattern produced by Kim's North Korea, Milosevic's Yugoslavia,
Saddam's Iraq, and now most adroitly by the Ayatollah Khamenei's
and Mahmoud Ahmedinejad's Iran. It has become the dictators'
diplomacy of choice; call it "dictaplomacy."

The Islamic Republic of Iran is a true revolutionary power.
Its central theme has been its relentless attacks, in words and
deeds, on the international system. As Kissinger wrote about
the Soviet Union, "whenever there exists a power which con-
siders the international order or the manner of legitimizing it
oppressive, relations between it and other powers will be revolutionary." This, as Iranian leaders have made clear, is the case
with the Islamic Republic and world order; it is the system
which must go for, as Kissinger noted, "the point is not that it
feels threatened—such feeling is inherent in the nature of
international relations based on sovereign states—*but that nothing can reassure it.*"

From the global point of view, the stakes are enormous. If the Islamists can defeat the Middle Eastern states that seek to reform and work within the international system, we will be faced with another world war. Like the cold war, it will be a war launched by a revolutionary ideology that aims to destroy the international state system and replace it with one of its own.

CENTERS OF GRAVITY

World order and its chief protector—the United States—need a concept. One may be found in the classic strategist Carl von Clausewitz's *Center of Gravity*, which the Defense Department defines as "the source of power that provides moral or material strength, freedom of action, or will to act." The task is to identify where an adversary's center of gravity is located and try to neutralize or redirect it—and at the same time to recognize our own center or centers of gravity and make the best use of them.

President George W. Bush's 2002 National Security Strategy was de facto a "center of gravity" approach, calling for "the transformation of the Greater Middle East," which was a summary way of saying that the Arab-Islamic region-culture-society had been moving in the wrong direction for decades, away from the international order and with the potential to drop out of it and go into violent opposition entirely. With the end of the cold war and the rise of Islamism, it was vital to understand how much the health of Islamic civilization mattered to the United States and to international security. Apparently out of fear of being accused of fomenting a "clash of civilizations" or being thought "anti-Muslim," the administration never clearly explained its approach or tried to educate the public about it. Nonetheless, the Bush years may be characterized as an attempt to shore up international order by promoting democratization within the regimes of the region and by shoring up the sovereign state as the basic building block of international relations there.

The weightiest center of gravity to be removed as the twenty-first century opened was Saddam Hussein's dictatorship. It was essential to end Saddam's dictatorship and central role as the region's most prominent adversary of the international system. The transformation of the greater Middle East was inconceivable as long as Saddam's Iraq remained as the geostrategic linchpin and psychological kingpin of radical Arab scorn for good international citizenship.

On the deepest level, the Bush strategy recognized that the international state system was *our* fundamental center of gravity and had to be shored up—and that the region of urgency was the Middle East.

In his State of the Union address of 2004, President Bush described it clearly:

> As long as the Middle East remains a place of tyranny, despair and anger, it will continue to produce men and movements that threaten the safety of America and our friends. So America is pursuing a forward strategy of freedom in the greater Middle East. We will challenge the enemies of reform, confront the allies of terror, and expect a higher standard from our friends . . . We have no desire to dominate, no ambitions of empire. Our aim is a democratic peace.

Every item on the Bush strategic agenda related to this strategy. They included pressuring Iran to abandon its "Dr. Jekyll and Mr. Hyde" strategy and to act as a responsible state in the system; helping Lebanon return to sovereign territorial integrity free of Syrian intervention; and urging reforms on Saudi Arabia, Egypt, and others in the Arab League of States in order to strengthen their legitimacy in the eyes of their own people. Bush's agenda also called for encouraging the rising Gulf States' deeper integration into the international state system and facilitating the goal of a "two-state solution" for Israel and Palestine.

The system is far from perfect, and international thinkers have longed to replace it. But it is all that we have at present, and history teaches us that we should shore it up, defend it, and make it work as best we can. We are not the ones to argue the demerits of Islamist positions; that is for non-Islamist Muslims to do, and mainstream Muslim arguments against Islamist views have been well-stated, as in Khaled Abou El-Fadl's *The Great Theft: Wrestling Islam Away From the Extremists.*

Our intellectual formulations need to be made on another level, to explain the vital importance of the international state system as a pragmatic mechanism for cross-civilizational interaction.

Keeping our focus on the necessity to shore up the established *procedural* international system, we can locate six issues on which our centers of gravity and those of Islamists are at odds: legal, military, the state, women, democracy, and nuclear weapons.

Legal: The terror-using combatants who violate every law of war as a matter of policy certainly are a center of gravity for Islamism. The fact that the established laws of war of the international system were designed for state-to-state conflict and not for insurgent warfare has posed a moral dilemma for our armed forces in parallel with its military challenges. For several years the United States has been making uneven efforts to cope with this situation.

Legally, it has been increasingly clear since 2001 that the protections provided by the several layers of the Geneva conventions assume that wars are fought by professional armies fielded by legitimate states in the international state system; they were not drafted in contemplation of the kind of enemy combatants we face in ongoing wars today. In desperation, the best efforts of the U.S. government to navigate through these legal shoals have produced no solutions, and little or no understanding of the unique nature of the challenge from the media or expert commentators. As former Attorney General Michael Mukasy stated, "The civilized world has tried over several hundred years to establish rules of warfare so that [soldiers of a professional army] are treated as prisoners of war when captured. Those who follow none of these rules are treated as war criminals, not as ordinary defendants accused of ordinary crimes and entitled to far more robust protection than war criminals. Congress recognized this when it passed the 2006 Military Commissions Act to deal with Islamist terrorism; disregarding that statute is lawless. Moreover, giving those who violate the laws of war more protection than is accorded those who follow such rules turns those rules and their underlying morality on their head." Mukasy's analysis explains the confusion now surrounding every aspect of taking and holding those captured on the battlefields or in terrorist operations within civil society. The balance between prisoner rights and

societal defense has not been located. Several layers and categories of American institutions continue to try to find ways to adapt
the laws of war and prisoners to deal properly with illegal combatants without going so far, as has recently been the case, as
granting them even more privileges than legal prisoners of war
under the traditional system. An entirely new, internally coherent and internationally understood body of law must be created
to update the international legal system.

Military: Military theorist Carl von Clausewitz's dictum is
that the supreme act of judgment is to understand what kind of
war you are fighting. One way to get at this in today's upside-
down cultural context would be to reject advice frequently
heard from the politically correct. For example:

- "There is no military solution." Wrong: the first order of
  business in winning a war is to kill the enemy fighters.
  Much beyond this will be needed, but to declare that
  there is no military solution is to start down the road to
  defeat.
- "Killing enemy fighters only recruits more to their
  cause." Wrong: potential recruits, when they know
  they are likely to die in battle, are more likely to remain
  "potential." Much has been made of Islamists who "love
  death" as a way to a blissful afterlife, but the terror wars
  have revealed that those in this category are few in
  number and serve as pawns in the hands of leaders who
  have no intention of arranging their own martyrdom.
- "Counter-terrorism (CT) and counter-insurgency
  (COIN) are the two options, and COIN is the one to

employ." Wrong: Until 2009 the strategy mainly was counter-terrorism, concentrating on killing enemy fighters. The massive 2010 Wikileaks promulgation of classified military-to-military communications revealed that counter-insurgency—i.e., regarding people to be the decisive "terrain" and working to build the economy, rule of law, and good governance on a regional basis—is indispensable. But both CT and COIN are needed, not only in parallel but also in tandem; they are preconditions for any parallel diplomatic effort.

- "Deadlines put vital pressure on our partners (in Afghanistan and Iraq) to get serious about taking the decisions needed to enable them to run their countries themselves." Wrong: Deadlines for U.S. withdrawal, if not conditions-based, are messages to all concerned that the Americans are preparing to give up and get out. Then, out of fear that the future belongs to the dictators, terrorists, and Islamists, our partners will start making their deals with the enemy.
- "We don't do nation-building." Right: No one can build a nation but the people of that nation. But we can, and must, build *states*.

The State, within the international state system, is another center of gravity. Most major wars of the modern era, in one way or another, have been ideologically driven assaults against the procedural international system, aimed at destroying and replacing it. The cold war was the greatest of these threats so far. Despite much post-cold-war damage done to the system, not least by critics among the intelligentsia of the West, the international state system remains the only tested and effective global arrangement available. The European Union's experiment appears to be receding into more traditional state-like governance. And it remains the case that every part of the Arab-Islamic region of the world is under the governance of a state that at least nominally is or seeks to be a legitimate member of the system. The most important influence on Muslim politics has not been Islam but the structures and mechanisms of each country's Westphalian-style state. Every key aspect of American, allied, and United Nations policy—political, social, and military—is aimed at restoring, shoring up, or achieving sound statehood across the Middle East.

One of the Islamists' main centers of gravity is rejection of the state as un-Islamic. Beyond their theological stance is a new perception of the power of statelessness. Electronic networks are arising outside of state control. Weapons of disruption and destruction capable of severely damaging a major state are now available to marginal non-state groups and individuals. Unlike a state, a decentralized, dispersed, and internationally non-responsible group can avoid the legal and financial burdens of statehood and the deterrable position of the possessor of sovereign territory. The desirability of not being a state has been spreading.

We need to support those Muslim-governed states that wish to remain and strengthen their roles as citizens in good standing in the international system against their enemies who promote the Islamist ideology of the state as a theological abomination.

And we need to provide good arguments for use against Islamists in revealing the state to be a procedural unit of organization, in no way a threat or alternative to Islam. Without a procedural and religiously neutral state that enables freedom of belief and expression, there is no possibility of successful development under the aegis of any religion, and no possibility of peace within or between religious communities. Islam and the procedural secular state require each other. It should be noted that the huge annual pilgrimage to Mecca—the *hajj*—is an international system that depends on states making procedural decisions enacted through international organizations. Overseen by the Organization of the Islamic Conference, the *hajj* system fits well into the established international system of states.

It is important to understand that the Islamist rejection of the state as the basic entity of the international state system is accompanied by Islamist calls for a "sharia state" to replace it. This Islamist concept of the state is not capable of being absorbed into an accommodation with the established state system. It is the opposite of the procedural Westphalian state; it is an idea of the sacred in political form. Pluralism is anathema to the Islamist state; its logical consequence would be a single *al Nizam al-Islami*, a single Islamist governing system for the world.

The Islamic Republic of Iran's center of gravity is the political theory invented by the Ayatollah Khomeini for his revolution of 1979 to combine theological absolutism with the powers of a sovereign state, the *velayat-e Faqih*. Iran's current "Supreme Guide," the Ayatollah Khamenei, in effect is saying, like Louis XIV, *"L'état, c'est moi."* Across the border in Iraq, the quiet presence of the Ayatollah Ali al-Sistani is a steady rebuke to the Iranian experiment, standing for the earlier-established Shia recognition that when religious leaders occupy positions of governmental responsibility, the unavoidably distasteful realities of politics will eventually taint and diminish the stature of the clerics. The Iranian center of gravity therefore is gravely compromised. The "rule of the jurisconsult" seems destined to fail, either being subsumed under a brutal and greedy authoritarianism, or transformed by the will of the people into a polity compatible with the international state system.

The Israeli-Palestinian conflict is now being addressed at a new and deeper level because of the importance of the state.

In 1979 Egypt and Israel recognized each other as legitimate states and signed a peace treaty. Recognizing that states can make peace only with other states in the international state system, Egypt took on the role of state negotiator with Israel on behalf of the Palestinians, who did not have a state. But after Islamists murdered President Sadat, Egypt dropped its role as state negotiator. Jordan then took up that role but dropped it in 1988. Since that time, negotiations have made no authentic breakthrough because there has been no state partner to sit across the table from the State of Israel.

But now the picture holds some new possibilities. The U.S. war in Iraq eliminated a rogue state that repeatedly disrupted progress toward peace. And "Operation Iraqi Freedom" has had an impact all across the region; today people in the Middle East can see that change for the better is not impossible. For the first time in the history of the Israeli-Palestinian conflict, following the initiative of Crown Prince, now King, Abdullah of Saudi Arabia, the Arab League of States has indicated a readiness to recognize a peace agreement reached between the State of Israel and a State of Palestine. This agreement would support both as permanent, legitimate states in the Middle East and in the international state system.

Despite constant claims that "the peace process" has failed and the situation gone backwards, years of negotiating effort have made some significant progress. The outlines of an agreement are now well known to those involved: the Israeli government and the Palestinian Authority, Egypt, Saudi Arabia, and Jordan, and the "Quartet"—the United States, the European Union, Russia, and the United Nations. An agreed document offers a possibility for the establishment of a Palestinian State, not at the end of the negotiations but in the midst of the effort. That would mean a Palestinian State partner with which the State of Israel could conclude the negotiations. The Palestinians would have more leverage and the Israelis would have more confidence that their negotiating partner could deliver on the deal that is made. This would be necessary but not sufficient unless the Arab states, perhaps in the form of the Arab League, follow through on their promised support for a two-state Israel-Palestine outcome.

Most important in a political-security-psychological sense is that the Middle East narrative may be changing from one in which "the plight of the Palestinians" is all that the Arab world cares about to one in which the rise of the revolutionary Islamist regime in Iran promoting terrorism, exacerbating the Shia-Sunni divide, and relentlessly pursuing nuclear weapons has become the major concern of the Arab regimes. This major narrative shift was reversed when President Obama, upon entering office, focused his demands on Israel first, in the form of insisting on a total settlements freeze, something through which the negotiating process had long before navigated. This was exacerbated by the Obama administration's return to the old claim that an Israeli-Palestinian solution held the key to all the region's problems, starting with the danger from Iran. Long and hard work was required to repair the damage done by this American blunder. There are so many positive factors for diplomacy to work with, and the growing danger from Iran and other radical Islamists is so obvious, that such repairs are imperative.

> The enemies of the state and of the international state system will step up their efforts to disrupt progress toward peace. The Islamists—and this camp includes Iran, al-Qaeda, Hezbollah, and Hamas—do not accept the existence of the State of Israel and will try to crush any incipient State of Palestine because nothing could be worse for the Islamists than the achievement of a two-state solution: the State of Israel and a State of Palestine.

Women. Centers of gravity at opposite poles are exemplified by the role of women in American life and in Islamist culture. The American attitude was stated by Tocqueville in perhaps the most famous sentence of *Democracy in America*:

> If I were asked to what do I attribute the
> great power and success of America I
> would answer,
> 'To the strength of the American woman.'

The situation of women's rights and roles in the United States is particularly evident in the advances registered since the women's revolution of the 1960s and 1970s.

In contrast, the status of women in the Arab-Islamic world is a constant source of dispute and controversy. The Arab-American legal philosopher Khaled Abou El Fadl points to the concept of *fitna*, or sexual endangerment, and notes the discrepancy between Quranic prescriptions which are designed to protect women and radical Islamist prohibitions which, perhaps as vestiges of pre-Islamic tribal society, seem to regard any exposure of women to the vicissitudes of ordinary life as opening up dire threats to the entire family as well as risks of civic and societal disruption. As one Arab social scholar put it, the man's honor is primarily defined by the conduct of his womenfolk. Therefore, the woman's honor becomes the primary business of the man, who must see to it that it is not violated. He has to guard it, for if it is besmirched, the stigma of immoral behavior falls on him and society at large will hold him accountable. Today, the results of this belief have produced not only "honor killings" of daughters by fathers governed by some pre-modern tribal law, but also such cases as the girls who, while attempting to escape the flames of a dormitory fire in Saudi Arabia, were forced back into the burning building to their deaths by the authorities because they were "not properly covered" to appear in public.

The wider implications of this condition of women in the Muslim world were detailed in the major study issued by the United Nations in 2002 under the title *Arab Human Development Report*. The AHDR is an unsparing diagnosis of the failure of the Arab world to keep pace with other nations in an era of globalization and interdependence. The reasons, stated simply, are the lack of freedom to acquire knowledge and to express ideas, and the denial of women's rights.

It did not take the AHDR to launch efforts to lift restrictions on women in Arab-Islamic regions. Some signs, if still minor, continue to accumulate of widening opportunities for women in education, employment, everyday living, and even politics. But the center of gravity still holds sway among Islamists and holds powerful leverage over sections of Muslim society not directly under Islamist control. There is slowly growing recognition that the authentic teachings of the Quran and Hadith have had to be manipulated by radical interpretations in order to provide a spurious theological cover for practices that are no more divinely decreed than was the practice of foot binding in pre-modern China.

Evidence of changing attitudes was the lead taken by women in the Tehran protests against the flawed and unfree presidential election of June 2009. Even covered women openly challenged men to do more, to stand up against the religious authorities. Such actions turn the Islamist cultural context inside out through their refusal to continue to acquiesce in what one demonstrator called "gender apartheid." But the women's rights movements of America have done little or nothing to support them.

American efforts to support this movement might take as a model the effort of Secretary of State George P. Shultz with Mikhail Gorbachev in the mid-1980s, a series of talks later called "the classroom in the Kremlin." The effort to persuade the Soviet leader was based not on philosophy or principle or rights but clearly and simply on the pragmatic reality that a Soviet society that continued to curtail freedoms of thought, speech, and individual enterprise could not possibly be successful or even keep pace as the rest of the world adapted and contributed to the information revolution and the potential for prosperity it offered. An even more compelling argument can be made to those in the Middle East who suppress the talents of half their population. But America should never back away from the higher moral cause involved as President Obama did in his National Security Strategy of 2010, which stated America's support for women's rights but conspicuously refused to list them under "universal rights," apparently out of fear of being contradicted by Islamists.

Democracy. The few basic procedural elements of the Westphalian system originally did not include democracy. Although Athens in antiquity provided rich examples for assessing the value of democracy in governance, it was not until the nineteenth century that Tocqueville's perception of an 800-year-long movement toward democracy as a "force of history" perhaps was warranted. And it was not until President Wilson spoke of "making the world safe for democracy" and put forward an international action plan calling for national self-determination based on the democratically expressed will of the people that democracy began to take hold on the world's consciousness. Democracy and America became inextricably linked. Democracy is America's center of gravity. Unless America stands for and promotes democracy, it cannot be true to its most elemental national character.

Not only did the Arab Middle East resolutely remain the one region of the world without a single democratic government, it also saw democracy discredited in the Middle East by its use as a cloak of legitimacy for autocratic regimes posing as legitimately elected governments.

The rise of Islamism further damaged the idea of democracy by asserting it to be wholly incompatible with *sharia*. In a democracy, elected representatives of the people would pass laws that would govern citizens' lives. But the only law, Islamists said, was God's law; therefore to democratize would be to attempt to destroy Islam.

President Bush, after 9/11, seeing the necessity to transform the Middle East in the direction of good governance, openly promoted democracy. While this gave heart to reformers and youth, gained some positive results in Lebanon, and brought the Arab world its first-ever democracy in post-Saddam Iraq, Bush's pro-democracy efforts also brought Islamists to power. These armed parties, once in office, would turn democracy into "one man, one vote, one time," i.e., just another road to entrenched oppression. In the United States, intellectuals were quick to denounce President Bush, disparage democracy as "unexportable" and "non-imposable," and call for a return to an American foreign policy based on hard-headed national interest rather than "Wilsonian idealism." This turn away from democracy as central to American foreign policy was institutionalized in President Obama's National Security Strategy of 2010 which made clear that while the United States would welcome democratic changes abroad, America would no longer actively promote it. As the columnist Anne Applebaum wrote, "The subsequent failure of Iraq to metamorphose overnight into the Switzerland of the Middle East is cited as an example of why democracy should never be pushed or promoted. This silly argument has had a strong echo: since becoming president, Barack Obama has shied away from the word democracy in foreign contexts—he prefers 'our common security and prosperity'—as if [democracy] might be some dangerous Bushism."

How can the United States strengthen its democratic center of gravity under these disadvantageous conditions? By explaining that democracy over the course of the twentieth century became an accepted addition to the international state system. The United Nations Charter, as drafted in 1945, did not contain the word "democracy"; but in the post-cold-war period, democracy became an integral part of the formal structure of international affairs openly authorized and called for in U.N. Security Council resolutions. This was, in a sense, an affirmation of Winston Churchill's statement: "Democracy is the worst form of government except for all the others." When constructing a new polity from the ground up, legitimacy can only be gained when the source of governmental authority is grounded in the free expression of the will of the people.

Alexis de Tocqueville in *Democracy in America* wrote that "Muhammad brought down from heaven and put into the Koran not religious doctrines only, but political maxims, criminal and civil laws, and scientific theories. . . . That alone, among a thousand reasons, is enough to show that Islam will not be able to hold its power long in ages of enlightenment and democracy." Tocqueville says this out of his recognition that the modern international system, with democracy as a part of it, is procedural, not substantive—and he seems to be saying that Islam is not only substantive, but dogmatically and aggressively so.

In contrast, democracy and the Westphalian system in which it operates neither require nor challenge any substantive commitment—ideological, religious, or otherwise—from its members. It requires only that each member adhere to a minimal number of practices and procedures that make it possible for states and other international entities to engage in working relationships even though they may be committed to vastly different substantive doctrines and objectives.

Thus, contrary to President Bush's often-stated belief that democracy is "a God-given right" when it comes to international affairs, democracy is simply the only reliably practical way to provide legitimacy and achieve results. Only democracy produces the "transparency" that economies require to avoid corruption. Only democracy keeps open the flow of information required to operate a modern society. As the economist Amartya Sen famously declared years ago, "No democratic country has ever suffered a famine," and as Friedrich Hayek explained, democracy is in this sense methodological; the best information utilized in the best way is the information possessed by each single individual. A crowd can empty a stadium more efficiently than any "authoritative" set of directions imposed from above.

Argued this way, America's center of gravity can be shown to be in the Arab-Islamic world's best interests and in no way incompatible with Islam. Out of the series of anti-regime protests

by peoples across the region in 2011, ideas and actions compatible with democratization are under way, providing hope for the
transformation of the greater Middle East.

The question of democracy will be a test, not for Islamism, but
for Islam itself, to show that Tocqueville—who almost never puts
a foot wrong—in this case is mistaken. Islamic practices in a
democracy would join other religions in political action and
debate over how far religion should go beyond private practice
to display itself in the public square.

Nuclear weapons. A major center of gravity of the international state system is the doctrine of collective security, which
ever since the end of the First World War has been the mechanism, in the words of the U.N. Charter, for "the maintenance
of international peace and security." Collective security, however, has shown itself to be a flawed tool in practice. It can work
well in dealing with minor to mid-level challenges to security,
but has stalled again and again when a truly hard case is brought
to the United Nations Security Council.

The Iranian regime clearly is aware of collective security's
ineffective record and has played the international community's
hopes against its inadequacies in a stylized dance for nearly three
decades in its goal of producing missile-deliverable nuclear
weapons. Iran's manipulation of the international system in this
regard has succeeded brilliantly to date.

Nuclear weapons when possessed will become a new center
of gravity for Iran, undergirding and dramatically accelerating
all of its Islamist objectives. The possession of an "Islamic
bomb" has been heralded for years as an ultimate source of
power, prestige, and political ascendancy in the Muslim world;

for the sole *Islamist* power to gain nuclear weapons capability would transform the Greater Middle East in exactly the opposite direction from that sought by the international system and the United States.

The Nuclear-Free World project is aimed at approaching an "end state" which would blend and update the key elements of the 1946 Acheson-Lilienthal Report (international control of fissile material) and the "grand bargain" of the 1968 Non-Proliferation Treaty (non-nuclear states will remain so and nuclear states will reduce their stockpiles). This ambitious project, led by George Shultz, Henry Kissinger, former senator Sam Nunn, and former secretary of defense William Perry, will require an entirely transformed geopolitical context from that which exists today. Halting the Islamic Republic of Iran's nuclear weapons program therefore is a precondition for progress on the Nuclear-Free World project.

A multilateral collective security effort has been under way for several years now, involving both offers of beneficial engagement with Iran (diplomacy) and sanctions (strength) to pressure Iran to alter course if it will not engage constructively with negotiators. On several occasions in the past the multilateral negotiators (Britain, France, Germany, Russia, the United Nations, and the United States) have set "or else" deadlines for Iran, only to postpone or abandon them when Iran has defied the date certain. The record is one of collective security failing to deal with the hardest cases. As a center of gravity of the international system, Iran has pushed the system to what might be its moment of truth.

The doctrine of collective security was designed to replace that of the balance of power as the primary means of maintaining

international peace and security, it having been felt that the First
World War had in some major way been caused by inherent
dangers in the balance-of-power concept. Today, the Nuclear-
Free World project could be interpreted as an attempt to shape
a new geopolitical context which would transcend or replace
collective security as the central mechanism for maintaining
international peace and security. It is, therefore, an initiative of
significant potential consequence.

The Acheson-Lilienthal plan failed because the geopolitical-
strategic context—the emerging cold war—would not permit it.
Today's emerging geopolitical-strategic context is being shaped
by Islamism with the Islamic Republic of Iran as the focus. It will
not, as now conducted, permit the creation of a new geopolitical-
strategic context other than that which it intends for Islamism.

The Nuclear-Free World end state is years away. The collective security challenge by Iran to the international system's
center of gravity is now.

Values. America's strongest center of gravity is our values.
We can now begin to realize that the values America has stood
for over the generations, and the regulations and understandings
evolved from them, are being turned into weapons against us.

During the 2008 election campaign, candidates and commentators often called the war in Afghanistan the right war, a
war of necessity, as opposed to the war in Iraq, a bad war of
choice. But once the White House changed hands, frustration
over the Afghan war mounted in the Congress, the media, and
the new administration. Those who shaped U.S. foreign policy
in earlier generations would say that America cannot afford to
lose another war, especially one with so many implications for

regional and international security and world order itself. But the mood is growing that Afghanistan is a war that cannot be won; that we should close it out and focus attention on our domestic agenda. This is the latest in a pattern that runs back to the Vietnam War, or even to the Korean War. Today, it is a problem of asymmetries.

A history of world civilization could be based on asymmetries.

From antiquity through early modern times, the powerful ruled the powerless, the haves over the have-nots. In Thucydides' *Peloponnesian War*, the Athenians tell the Melians, "The strong exact what they can; the weak concede what they must."

In the late nineteenth century, a new mentality began to take hold: a widening effort to close the asymmetry gap by constricting the use of force in war and by developing new protections for civilians, combatants, and POWs. As we have seen, an important moment came in the 1870–71 Franco-Prussian War when the use of illegal combatants, the *francs-tireurs*, was immediately denounced and the wrongdoers subjected to summary punishment. The moral paradigm of civilized conduct put the blame squarely on those who deliberately rejected professional military requirements and endangered civilian populations. That was then, but not the way it is now.

In the twentieth century, the movement to close the asymmetry gap was largely led by the United States: in the political field, human rights; in the economic field, development assistance; in law, promotion of the military justice system to ensure that those who violate the laws of war are treated as war criminals, not as ordinary defendants. These and other gap-closing steps became required procedures adopted by the international state system. They established the standards for an international civilization.

But then the legal and moral restrictions that the stronger—particularly the United States—had imposed on themselves began to be used as a matter of "strategic tactics." The laws of war and Geneva Conventions, enhanced procedural safeguards, and deepening moral concerns for civilized conduct were in effect "weaponized" by insurgents. Terrorism—the deliberate use of civilian populations to advance radically violent causes—became the centerpiece of a war on world order.

The enemies of the international state system and, in effect, of civilized behavior, have found advantages in the fact of asymmetry. They use the ungoverned spaces of the world to gather, plan, and train for acts of violence against legitimate states and their populations—and do so in the service of a religiously inspired ideology aimed at destroying and replacing the established international state system. Their asymmetrical tactics are employed ceaselessly and successfully. Their view is that they do not have to win the war, they only have to not lose it, prolonging it until we grow impatient and politically dispirited, until our side begins to conclude that "this war cannot be won" and sets timelines for withdrawal.

Every category in the "center of gravity" section above is marked by dangerous asymmetry. The laws of war have been used as a cover for illegal combatants; civilians, rather than being protected by the system, become body shields for the killers. Statelessness flaunts its advantages over statehood; culture and dogma are cited as requiring unequal treatment of women; and democracy's guarantees of liberty and equality are said by autocrats to be destabilizing.

The most horrendous asymmetrical threat of all comes from the potential use of a nuclear weapon by an extremist group with "no known address" and which is therefore unreachable by strategies of deterrence. The relative success of asymmetrical methods by such ideologically driven terrorists can only tempt states that are adversarial to one another or to world order itself to devise ways to transfer nuclear weapons to their surrogates—euphemistically called "non-state actors"—in ways that are disavowable or so attenuated that a nuclear attack so arranged could not be traced in a timely way to the nuclear state in question. No program or approach has yet been created that can deal with such a threat within the time frame of the perceived danger.

Among the policies and techniques we have employed to cope with this shift in the balance of asymmetries are public diplomacy, state-building, counter-insurgency and counter-terrorism strategies, the new National Security Strategy of comprehensive no-fault diplomacy, and the range of military counter-measures from up-armoring vehicles to enhanced intelligence collection and analysis. In the hope of fending off legal challenges arising from the fact of asymmetry, we have deployed lawyers to advise our combat units on when and how and at whom to shoot. But the fundamental phenomenon of asymmetry has not been addressed in any effective way, nor have we any answer to the strange paradigm shift that has placed us at such a material and moral disadvantage.

America must not give up its values, nor retreat by declaring we will live up to them by practicing them only at home or by telling ourselves that our values are no more worthy than any others selected at random from the world's many cultures. The first step is to recognize the problem and then try to develop ways to deal with the exploitation of asymmetries by the enemies of world order.

CHAPTER SIX

In the Matter of Grand Strategy

T HE MODERN INTERNATIONAL STATE SYSTEM from Westphalia through the Enlightenment and into the twenty-first century is itself a grand strategy and a civilization. It is every civilization's *other* civilization, addressing a natural need, much as diverse species depend upon a common ecosystem. Those who can recognize this and take advantage of it will be the successful international citizens.

Islamic civilization entered the international system under duress. In its politico-economic form as a collection of sovereign states, Islam has been uneasy and far less successful than its pre-modern history would have indicated. To compensate, many Muslims have defined their differences and difficulties with the modern system in a rigidified, often radicalized, way, which only worsens their discomfort and performance in the contemporary world order.

A prominent aspect of the Westphalian system has been its relegation of religion to the margins of state-to-state world affairs. With the late twentieth-century rise of radical Islam,

religion has returned as a factor in international security, posing a fundamental challenge to both the champions and the
critics of the system.

As a grand strategy, the international system is grounded in
a single concept: it is procedural. It simplifies international
relations to a near minimum of non-substantive requirements—
an Occam's Razor for the world's nations. In this way the system proved flexible enough to accommodate the immense
variety of doctrines, beliefs, and practices of its globe-spanning
members. But a line must be drawn at some point. If political
positions become ideologies or religions become dogmas unable
to accommodate others, then they inevitably will be unable to
tolerate the system's procedural requirements; conflict, even
war, may be the consequence. This describes Islamism's threat to
world order today and its fundamental challenge to Westphalia's
objective of avoiding wars of religions.

All this has raised a question among some Muslims of
whether Islam can ever accommodate itself to the international
system yet remain true to itself. Islamists say no. But many
profound thinkers in Islam have advanced ideas in the affirma-
tive. The focus is on "secularism" and on what this concept
really means in world affairs today.

This has turned some serious and responsible people, Muslim
and non-Muslim, into amateur theologians in search of arguments about ways in which the twain can meet, about whether
Islam—and we're not talking about Islamists here—can be compatible and comfortable within the larger international state
system for world order.

One argument states that requiring an Islamic state to enforce *sharia* as a matter of state "is in fact promoting a European positivistic view of law and a totalitarian model of the state that seeks to transform society in its own image." Thus *sharia* imposed by the will of the regime in power cannot be the true law of Islam. It is not possible to apply *sharia* through the state; it can only be applied through acceptance by human beings (An-Na'im).

Another argument points out that the Prophet established at Medina a polity that separated matters of Islamic belief from the functions of the state. Muhammad "sat down with the city's fractious tribes to hammer out a covenant (later called the Pact—*kitab*—of Medina). This covenant made the city a confederacy, guaranteeing each tribe the right to follow its own religion and customs, imposing on all citizens rules designed to keep the overall peace, establishing a legal process by which the tribes settled purely internal matters themselves and ceded to Muhammad the authority to settle intertribal disputes. . . . Although this document has been called the first written constitution, it was really more of a multiparty treaty" (Ansary). Thus Muslims today should be willing and able to live their faith amidst those who follow other religions and customs.

Another version of the above argument, a kind of reverse spin, points out that the Quran demarcates two distinct periods: at Mecca, where the Faith was to be adopted through persuasion; and at Medina, where the Prophet began to carry the Message to the world by force of arms. Some Muslim scholars give precedence to the passages conveyed at Mecca, on the principle

that earlier texts carry more authority than later utterances, a
kind of "best evidence rule" for theologians.

Yet another view, from Egyptian theologian Ali Abd al-Raziq
(1888–1966), challenges the established doctrine that Islam
does not recognize the distinction between the sacred and the
profane, between spiritual and temporal, between church and
state: "If such a characteristic has been peculiar to Islam since
its origins, why has it been necessary to recall, reformulate or
indeed rediscover it from new standpoint and in new terms
throughout the course of the twentieth century?" Abd al-Raziq
reviewed the corpus of texts defining Islam, i.e., the Quran and
Hadith, and found "no injunction or any indication whatsoever
for Muslims about any political system or order they should
adopt." All one finds in the texts is a certain number of recom-
mendations about morals in the widest sense, but no principles
of political life. Abd al-Raziq showed how a strictly political,
temporal power (the power set up after the Prophet's death)
"*annexes* religion and proceeds to invent a political system which
encompasses religion, converting it to a reserved domain under
its own control and for its own purposes." In our time this looks
like what has happened, *inter alia*, in Zia's Pakistan, Saddam's
Iraq, and Khomeini's Iran. Abd al-Raziq showed that "the political era begins with the death of the Prophet, thus taking away
the sacred aura from a period enshrined as a golden age." Thus,
"to use the term 'Islamic political regime' is a contradiction in
terms: there never has been and never could be such a thing"
(Abdou Filali-Ansari).

Such scholarly analyses as these four reveal that Islamic
regimes in our time, whether states or kingdoms or republics,

really are not examples of Islam's uniate melding of political and sacred power, but cases in which rulers have incorporated the faith as a way to complete their domination of the people. There is, Professor L. Carl Brown of Princeton wrote, "nothing exclusively 'Islamic' about this Muslim attitude toward politics any more than the politics of feudalism or of imperial Russia was distinctly 'Christian.' It is the political legacy of Muslims, not the theology of Islam, that is under consideration."

All these theological interpretations see the necessity for the state to be neutral regarding religious doctrine—something not unlike the "secular" or procedural character of the Westphalian system. As An-Na'im puts it,

> Secularism needs religion to provide a widely accepted source of moral guidance for the political community as well as to help satisfy and discipline the needs of believers within that community. Religion needs secularism to mediate relations among different communities (whether religious or antireligious or nonreligious) that share the same political space.

This sounds much like Tocqueville, who finds at the core of democracy in America the conviction that religion and liberty are compatible: that liberty sees religion as the cradle of its development while religion sees liberty as the arena for its practice.

Thus, says Brown, the "historical storehouse of Islamic thought concerning politics contains themes that could be utilized by modern Muslim thinkers to present an Islam quite different from what the radical Islamists advance." Signal among these "is the venerable Muslim resistance to permitting government to impose religious doctrine . . . the deep-seated sense that the individual's Islamic credentials are to be judged by God alone, not by other men, even less by government." This is particularly relevant "to those who assert that there is not—cannot be—any separation between religion and the state in Islam. To say this is to ignore much of what has actually happened throughout Islamic history."

What about Islamic values? The most comprehensive, learned, challenging statement from the Islamic standpoint has been made by Ali A. Allawi in his powerful book *The Crisis of Islamic Civilization*, a work that unflinchingly takes on the question of whether Islam, rightly understood and practiced by believers, can ever be compatible with responsible citizenship within the international state system and community.

Tracking Allawi's argument across his book, a logic chain emerges:

1. The core of Islamic civilization is different both from other civilizations and from the dominant globalizing world. The difference is the "transcendental element"; Islam cannot enter modernity if this element is lost. If the concept of the state displaces this element, a state "is simply unthinkable to a Muslim." Still, Allawi grants, the state "is unlikely to be replaced as the primary political unit for Muslims in the short term." This is in part because the 1979 Iranian Revolution shifted the Muslim world toward an open association of Islam with the modern state.

2. Secularism is a trap. The entire inheritance of the Judeo-Christian tradition seemed to end up traduced

by the secular state. Modern secularism is a form of war against God—yet "the secular make-over of Islam has virtually become a national security issue for the United States." Similarly, calling upon Islam to reform, i.e., undergo its own version of the Enlightenment or the Reformation, is a recipe for self-destruction. Those Islamic thinkers, such as the contemporary Iranian Abd el-Karim Soroush, who come close to finding a natural affinity between a democratic sensibility and a religious morality are simply opening the way for Islam to be overwhelmed by the profane world. Muslim democracy is a pathway to a secular and ultimately Western definition of the political.

3. Of all the world's civilizations, only Islam has had no state on the world stage. This absence of territorial power has rendered Islam powerless in an international system of large states. "The kind of power that Islam may exert on the global scene is directly related to whether that power is connected to a state champion or whether it will be expressed some other way." At present, a state actor is a precondition for admission to the world's upper reaches of power wielders. So the demand for an *Islamic* state is fundamental to the future of Islam and the appropriate government for Muslims. In the past, Muslims living under non-Islamic rule or rule by non-Muslims "was a rare and unhappy experience." At the same time, the concept of the caliphate is an idea that has refused to go away from Muslim minds. But the caliphate is unlikely to be resuscitated.

4. So, Allawi says, there are only two possible outcomes:
   either shrink Islam and relegate it to the private sphere,
   making it like the non-established religions of the
   modern era, or create "an alternative modernity." The
   former, a privatization of Islam, will never be accepted,
   Allawi says. Muslims must have a public manifestation
   of Islam in daily life.

The latter outcome, says Allawi, will depend upon "whether
Muslims want to create and dwell in a civilizational space which
grows out of their own beliefs without disrupting the world of
others." But that civilizational space will have to reclaim those
parts of the Islamic public space conceded to other worldviews
over past centuries.

It is not easy to find any room in Allawi's logic chain for
mutually respectful accommodation between Islam and the way
the rest of the world has organized itself to work—procedurally,
not substantively—across the modern centuries. At the end,
Allawi seems to hold out a ray of hope by pointing to al-Ghazali,
"Algazel" to the West, Islam's greatest scholarly figure. The
charge that his turn to the transcendent ended rational discourse
for Islam—see page 15 in Chapter One—is a gross calumny
which ever since has wrongly defined Islam. In fact, says Allawi,
al-Ghazali produced a synthesis of reason and revelation. The
need, which no modern movement has filled, is some way to
integrate the sacred and profane in daily life.

In 1892, more than a century before Allawi's reappraisal of
al-Ghazali, an American theologian, Duncan Black MacDonald
of the Hartford Seminary, considered al-Ghazali's thought to be

a bridge between East and West. He considered al-Ghazali to be "the equal of Augustine" and "the most sympathetic figure in the history of Islam."

As the politico-religious historical storehouse of Islamic thought can be tapped for an alternative modernity, so politico-theological thought in the West is reassessing the modern age—supposedly one of "disenchantment," as Max Weber described it—and finding a new secular-sacred connection.

RELIGION IN WORLD ORDER REVISITED

All parties agree about the role of religion in the pre-modern age: it was pervasive, central, powerful, and generally respected as a given of the human condition.

The modern world, in sharp contrast, has defined itself *against* religion. Among the elites, religion is to be neutralized, marginalized, excluded, and often derided.

As the modern world began in the sixteenth and seventeenth centuries, religious conflicts and confrontations were exacerbated. Modern politics began, the consensus says, with Machiavelli's *The Prince* of 1513. The shock that this small book administered to religion still reverberates. Machiavelli took the word "virtue" and emptied it of both classical and Christian meaning, refilling the word with meanings dedicated to the getting and keeping of power in the "City of Man"—no more preoccupation with Augustine's *City of God*.

The Thirty Years' War ended in the 1648 Treaty of Westphalia which, as reiterated throughout this book, aimed to neutralize religion as a source of animosity among states. The modern international system expected that states, whatever the religion professed by their rulers or people, would deal with one another on a secular basis.

Political measures to diminish the role of religion were the beginning; philosophical contributions added to the effect. "Enlightenment," Kant wrote in 1784, "is man's leaving his self-imposed immaturity. Immaturity is the incapacity to use one's intelligence without the guidance of another." Kant made it clear that he was speaking of the need of modern people to turn away from churches and clergymen and the "superstitions" they promote.

Then came the Revolution, and the religion of the Revolution, or the Revolution as religion, or the Revolution as a substitute for religion. Jacques-Louis David's *The Death of Marat* was put on display in Paris on October 16, 1793, the day that Marie Antoinette went to the guillotine. Terror had been made the "order of the day," and Marat had urged the most radical killing of all. Marat *is* "The People"; he *is* "the Revolution." He is in a medicinal bath because of the skin disease he contracted while hiding in the sewers of Paris. The body of the people is and must be cleansed, purified. Marat will die for the people— stabbed by Charlotte Corday as he bathes—in order to save them. David paints Marat as a modern *pietà*: revolution as a substitute for religion.

The globalizing economy made its own contributions to the demise of religion. Jonathan Swift provides a glimpse of this in *Gulliver's Travels* when Gulliver contrives to be excused from the requirements imposed by Japanese officials in Nagasaki that foreign commercial traders "trample on the crucifix," which all Christian businessmen willingly do, Gulliver ruefully notes.

Max Weber weaves this into "modernization theory." Simply put, as a nation—any nation—develops economically and enters the modern economy, its people will develop as well, losing interest in, and eventually turning away from, religion.

This modern assault on religion reaches its zenith with Friedrich Nietzsche, who argued that "the concepts Christianity uses to analyze moral experience . . . are entirely imaginary and psychologically pernicious." Nietzsche rejected Western civilization as polluted throughout by Christianity.

What effect did this disposal of religion have on lives in the modern age? The social philosopher Jürgen Habermas noted that since the close of the eighteenth century, modernity has weakened social bonding by a rationalizing process that evokes the need for something "equivalent to" the unifying power of religion.

What "equivalents"?

The "Legitimacy of the Modern Age" controversy (Hans Blumenberg versus Karl Löwith) dealt with the question of whether Marxism and its social welfare variations made up a substitute religion somewhat in the lineage of David's *Marat*. In this approach, heaven can be attained on earth in some future social utopia. Löwith argued that "the modern project" copies Christian eschatology; Blumenberg said no—it just fills the emptiness left by the departed faith. In a sense both come out on the same side: *modernity* is a religion.

Another "equivalent" was provided by Martin Heidegger: civilization has clouded our minds. The only hope is to go back beyond and before civilization, to the pre-Socratic Greek thinkers who may put us in touch with *Being*, an authenticity of blood and soil more profound than any religion. Heidegger's Nazism explains a great deal.

Then came the neo-pragmatists and neo-utilitarians, Richard Rorty and Peter Singer notable among them. "We are all anti-foundationalists now," they proclaimed. This seemed to carry original Enlightenment thinking to its logical consequence: reason above all. Daniel Dennett contributed to this approach via neo-Darwinism, "a universal acid" that corrodes and destroys every attempt to rely upon a foundation, a faith, or a "sky-hook," as he put it. But close attention to their work raises suspicions that they were smuggling contraband into their kingdoms, items that look very much like the elements of a religious faith.

Europe was to be another religion-equivalent, a near-perfect demonstration of Weber's modernization and economic development theory, the most developed part of the world, and therefore post-Christian. The new faith was to be Europe itself, and America its evil adversary, as Hannah Arendt announced in a lecture at Princeton in the mid-twentieth century.

So the modern world did away with religion. But, of course, it didn't. Out in the world beyond Western Europe, religion was vibrant and in many places dominant. And the international state system now confronts its first truly religion-driven war since 1648.

The Enlightenment's modern age not only wonderfully altered the human condition through near-miracles of science and technology, but also produced some of history's worst human and environmental horrors. A strong sense took hold in some parts of the West and non-West alike that secularist (from the Latin *seculum*, worldly), rationalist modernity had failed to provide a moral basis for politics and for life itself. Modernity's attempt to expel the divine sense of life—the so-called "disenchantment" of the world—and its lack of interest in questions of higher meaning only spurred religious feelings. While the Westphalian international system largely succeeded in curtailing major religious wars, religion did not wither away but in many places grew more intense under the destabilizing pressures of modernization and globalization. A new phenomenon arose: wars motivated by religious convictions were replaced by wars driven by ideologies—surrogates for religion—each aimed to oppose, undermine, destroy and replace the Westphalian system. The greatest of these was international communism, the latest is international Islamism.

The conventional admiration of the Enlightenment as "The Age of Reason" was vehemently challenged in 1947 by Max Horkheimer and Theodor W. Adorno in their *Dialectic of Enlightenment*, reprinted ever since, which attributed the worst horrors of the twentieth century to reason unconstrained by values. I knew Horkheimer in the early 1960s in Zürich, where I was the American vice consul who periodically had to certify his intention to keep his naturalized American citizenship. Horkheimer then aimed at creating, as Ali Allawi later put it, "an alternative modernity." This was resisted by Jürgen Habermas in "Reflections on a Remark by Max Horkheimer: To Seek an Unconditioned Meaning without God is a Pointless Undertaking," in which Habermas

unpersuasively argued that Enlightenment reason was sufficient unto itself.

Related to this have been claims that the "procedures" of the
modern international system are themselves derived from a
religious source of values. The state is not only, as Hegel
declared, the realization of the Spirit in the world, "the divine
idea as it exists on earth," but also represents the biblical idea
of "the nations" after Babel. Similarly, constructions such as
equal protection, due process, freedom for individual expression, and the conviction that sovereignty must reside in the
people may appear procedural when viewed through one lens,
but as God-given rights when seen from another angle. The
international legal concept of "the equality of states" ("a *profound* doctrine," Boutros-Ghali said to me) derived from a
transcendental belief. Only the idea of "the soul" can justify the
otherwise implausible view that individuals are free and equal;
and only a recognition that sovereignty is to the state as the
soul is to the body can explain the otherwise nonsensical
thought that Iceland and India are equals as states in the
United Nations General Assembly. So what on the surface
appears to be a secular age turns out to be deeply suffused with
a sacral sense of the human condition.

Against this background the philosopher Charles Taylor
declares that today's secular age has come about not as the result
of subtracting religion, but as a new phase in humanity's religious
evolution. Modernity has brought forward its own original spiritual content: benevolence, meliorism, and "an increasing aware-
ness of other cultures and traditions, and the cosmopolitanism

born of so many different cultures." Thus, argues Taylor, secularization has eliminated any *naïve* acceptance of religion; it offers a new field for religious exploration.

Al-Ghazali, who died in 1111, and Anselm, bishop of Canterbury, were contemporaries. For each, although a transcendent God cannot be known by rational insight alone, the will of God is never irrational. Something here may link the postmodern secular age with the pre-modern age of faith. The paradigm of religion versus secularism may be passing away. In the emerging paradigm there are Muslim commentators who regard the enforcement of a theo-ideology by governing authority to be in some sense blasphemous because those who administer it claim to know God's will, abolishing the freedom true faith requires. And from the other side can be heard the similar view that "religion ceases to be religion when its poetic authority is recast as civic authority."

The Job of the Bible and the Job of the Quran are vastly different. The Bible's Book of Job emphasizes narrative as a history across time. The Quran's revelations are arranged with no discernible narrative sequence, ahistorical and timeless, not dynamic. Yet they seem to share the message that no human causation or explanation will be found, that incomprehensible wonder—not imposed earthly doctrine—is prerequisite to faith.

This by no means is an argument for the convergence of disparate religions. Indeed, as James Carse states, the different religions are irreconcilable and comparative religion a misconceived project because one religion simply is not comparable to another.

What can be said is that a new mentality is emerging which begins to dissolve the conventional wisdom that a secular versus sacred confrontation is inevitable.

The test may come in political form. A contemporary Muslim thinker has said, echoing a common perception, that it is misleading to think of Islam as one in a class of Christianity, Judaism, Hinduism, etc. It is just as valid to consider Islam to be in a class with communism, democracy, and fascism because Islam is a *social project*, in Ali Allawi's description, ". . . a vast complex of communal purposes moving through time, driven by its own internally coherent assumptions." In contrast, a contemporary Christian thinker declares, "The Western faiths have moved away in modern times from believing that they had some superior insight into the concrete workings of politics and economics. Though some critics have seen this as a tacit admission of failure, in fact it shows a better understanding of the true mission."

The question comes down to democracy. If Islam indeed is "in a class with" democracy, then its dogmatic adherents must give way. The Islamist claim has been that the Islamic state must be the sole repository of truth and the only truly legitimate power on earth. That is incompatible with, and adversarial to, world order. The conventional Islamic claim has been that God's sovereignty and *sharia* would be violated if sovereignty were vested in the people and laws made by the people's democratically elected representatives. If, however, this is used to justify unchallengeable, unchangeable rule by a theocratic-autocratic government, then religion will be determined by civic authority and will cease to be religion. The word of God does not change, but interpretation of it does change, so no government should have a monopoly on its interpretation. "True" democracy—as a procedural mechanism in a procedural international state system—would provide for the dispersal of power and the circulation of power-holders and thus be not only compatible with but indispensible to "true" belief.

Epilogue

On the Road to Oxiana

Tabriz (4,500 feet) October 15

Christopher, at this stage, was reading in the back of the lorry, where his companions were a Teherani, an Isfahani, two muleteers, and the driver's assistant.

Teherani: What's this book?

Christopher: A book of history.

Teherani: What history?

Christopher: The history of Rum and the countries near it, such as Persia, Egypt, Turkey, and Frankistan.

Assistant (opening the book): Ya Ali! What characters!

Teherani: Can you read it?

Christopher: Of course. It's my language.

Teherani: Read it to us.

Christopher: But you cannot understand the language.

Isfahani: No matter. Read a little.

Muleteers: Go on! Go on!

Christopher: "It may occasion some surprise that the Roman pontiff should erect, in the heart of France, the tribunal from whence he hurled his anathemas against the king; but our surprise will vanish so soon as we form a just estimate of a king of France in the eleventh century."

Teherani: What's that about?

Christopher: About the Pope.

Teherani: The Foof? Who's that?

Christopher: The Caliph of Rum.

Muleteer: It's a history of the Caliph of Rum.

Teherani: Shut up! Is it a new book?

Assistant: Is it full of clean thoughts?

Christopher: It is without religion. The man who wrote it did not believe in the prophets.

Teherani: Did he believe in God?

Christopher: Perhaps. But he despised the prophets. He said that Jesus was an ordinary man (*general agreement*) and that Mohammad was an ordinary man (*general depression*) and that Zoroaster was an ordinary man.

Muleteer (*who speaks Turkish and doesn't understand well*): Was he called Zoroaster?

Christopher: No, Gibbon.

Chorus: Ghiboon! Ghiboon!

Teherani: Is there any religion which says there is no god?

Christopher: I think not. But in Africa they worship idols.

Teherani: Are there many idolators in England?

—Robert Byron, 1937

BIBLIOGRAPHY

Abou El Fadl, Khaled. *The Great Theft: Wrestling Islam from the Extremists.* Harper, 2005.

Achcar, Gilbert. *The Arabs and the Holocaust.* Trans. G. M. Goshgarian. Henry Holt, 2009.

Al-Ghazali, Abu Hamid Muhammed. *The Incoherence of the Philosophers.* Trans. Michael Marmura. Brigham Young University Press, 2000.

Allawi, Ali A. *The Crisis of Islamic Civilization.* Yale University Press, 2009.

Al-Radi, Selma. *The Amiriya in Rada: The History and Restoration of a Sixteenth-Century Madrasa in the Yemen.* Oxford University Press, 1999.

An-Na'im, Abdullahi. *Islam and the Secular State: Negotiating the Future of Shari'a.* Harvard University Press, 2008.

Ansary, Tamim. *Destiny Disrupted: A History of the World Through Islamic Eyes.* Public Affairs, 2009.

Arnold, Thomas W. *The Caliphate.* Oxford University Press, 1924.

Bar, Shmuel. *Warrant for Terror: The Fatwas of Radical Islam and the Duty to Jihad.* Hoover Institution, 2006.

Barany, Zoltan. "Authoritarianism in Pakistan." *Policy Review.* August & September 2009.

Bianchi, Robert. *Guests of God: Pilgrimage and Politics in the Islamic World.* Oxford University Press, 2004.

Bix, Herbert. *Hirohito and the Making of Modern Japan.* Harper Collins, 2000.

Bobbitt, Philip. *Terror and Consent: The Wars for the Twenty-First Century.* Allen Lane, 2008.

Brown, L. Carl. *Religion and State: The Muslim Approach to Politics.* Columbia University Press, 2000.

Brown, Peter. *Society and the Holy in Late Antiquity.* University of California Press, 1982.

Brumberg, Daniel. *Reinventing Khomeini: The Struggle for Reform in Iran.* University of Chicago Press, 2001.

Byron, Robert. *The Road to Oxiana.* Oxford University Press, 1982.

Calvert, John. *Sayyid Qutb and the Origins of Radical Islamism.* Columbia University Press, 2010.

Carse, James P. *The Religious Case Against Belief.* Penguin, 2008.

Cooper, Barry. *New Political Religions, or an Analysis of Modern Terrorism.* University of Missouri Press, 2005.

Curtis, Michael. *Orientalism and Islam: European Thinkers on Oriental Despotism in the Middle East and India.* Cambridge University Press, 2009.

Dalin, David and John F. Rothman. *Icon of Evil: Hitler's Mufti and the Rise of Radical Islam.* Random House, 2008.

Davies, Brian and Brian Leftow. *The Cambridge Companion to Anselm.* Cambridge University Press, 2004.

Diner, Dan. *Lost in the Sacred: Why the Muslim World Stood Still.* Trans. Steven Rendall. Princeton University Press, 2009.

Djait, Hichem. *Europe and Islam.* Trans. Peter Heinegg. University of California Press, 1985.

Elmarsafy, Ziad. *The Enlightenment Quran: The Politics of Translation and the Construction of Islam.* Oneworld, 2009.

Euben, Roxanne. *Enemy in the Mirror: Islamic Fundamentalism and the Limits of Modern Rationalism.* Princeton University Press, 1999.

Fairbank, John King, ed. *The Chinese World Order: Traditional China's Foreign Relations.* Harvard University Press, 1968.

Faroqhi, Suraiya. *The Ottoman Empire.* Trans. Shelley Frisch. Markus Wiener, 2009.

Faust, Drew Gilpin. *The Creation of Confederate Nationalism.* Louisiana State University Press, 1988.

Figes, Orlando. *Crimea: The Last Crusade.* Allen Lane, 2010.

Filali-Ansari, Abdou. "Islam and Secularism," in *Islam, Modernism, and the West.* Gema Martin Munoz, ed. I.B. Tauris. 1999.

Fradkin, Hillel, ed. *Current Trends in Islamist Ideology.* Vols. 1–10. Hudson Institute.

Fukuyama, Francis. *The End of History and the Last Man.* Free Press, 1992.

Fuller, Lon L. *The Morality of Law.* Yale University Press, 1964.

Furet, Francois. *A Critical Dictionary of the French Revolution.* Harvard University Press, 1989.

Gellner, Ernest. *Postmodernism, Reason and Religion.* Routledge, 1992.

Gillespie, Michael Allen. *The Theological Origins of Modernity.* University of Chicago Press, 2008.

Goffman, Daniel. *The Ottoman Empire and Early Modern Europe.* Cambridge University Press, 2002.

Gong, Gerrit W. *The Standard of "Civilization" in International Society.* Oxford University Press, 1984.

Grygiel, Jakub. "The Power of Statelessness." *Policy Review* No. 154, 2009.

Hanke, Lewis. *All Mankind is One: A Study of the Disputation Between Bartolomé de las Casas and Juan Ginés de Sepúlveda in 1550 on the Intellectual and Religious Capacity of the American Indians.* Northern Illinois University Press, 1974.

Heath, Ian and Michael Perry. *The Taiping Rebellion 1851–1866.* Osprey, 1994.

Herf, Jeffrey. *Nazi Propaganda for the Arab World.* Yale University Press, 2009.

Herman, Arthur. *Gandhi and Churchill.* Bantam Books, 2008.

Hodges, Richard and David Whitehouse. *Mohammed, Charlemagne, and the Origins of Europe: Archeology and the Pirenne Thesis.* Cornell University Press, 1983.

Hodgson, Marshall G.S. *The Venture of Islam: Conscience and History in a World Civilization.* Vol. 2 "The Expansion of Islam in the Middle Periods." University of Chicago Press, 1974.

Howard, Michael. *War and the Liberal Conscience.* Rutgers University Press, 1986.

Howland, Jacob. *Kierkegaard and Socrates: A Study in Philosophy and Faith.* Cambridge University Press, 2006.

Hutchins, Francis. *Illusion of Permanence: British Imperialism in India.* Princeton University Press, 1967.

———. *India's Revolution: Gandhi and the Quit India Movement.* Harvard University Press, 1973.

Jones, Dorothy V. *Code of Peace: Ethics and Security in the World of the Warlord States.* University of Chicago Press, 1989.

Kedourie, Elie. *The Chatham House Version and Other Middle-Eastern Studies.* University Press of New England, 1984.

Khaldun, Ibn. *The Muqaddimah: An Introduction to History.* Trans. Franz Rosenthal. Bollingen, 1969 (1377).

Korn, David A. *Assassination in Khartoum.* Indiana University Press, 1993.

Landau, Jacob M. *The Politics of Pan-Islam: Ideology and Organization.* The Clarendon Press, 1994.

Lassner, Jacob and Michael Bonner. *Islam in the Middle Ages: The Origins and Shaping of Classical Islamic Civilization.* Praeger, 2010.

Lewis, Bernard. *The Middle East and the West.* Weidenfeld and Nicolson, 1964.

———. *The Political Language of Islam.* University of Chicago Press, 1988.

Liu, Lydia H. *The Clash of Empires: The Invention of China in Modern World Making*. Harvard University Press, 2004.

Lybyer, Albert. *The Government of the Ottoman Empire in the time of Suleiman the Magnificent*. Harvard University Press, 1913.

Mackey, Sandra. *The Iranians: Persia, Islam and the Soul of a Nation*. Plume, 1998.

Manela, Erez. "Imagining Woodrow Wilson in Asia: Dreams of East-West Harmony and the Revolt Against Empire in 1919." *American Historical Review*. December 2006, 1327–1351.

Mazower, Mark. *Dark Continent: Europe's Twentieth Century*. Penguin, 1998.

McMeekin, Sean. *The Berlin-Baghdad Express: The Ottoman Empire and Germany's Bid for World Power, 1898–1918*. Allen Lane, 2010.

McNeill, William H. *The Rise of the West: A History of the Human Community*. University of Chicago Press, 1963.

McNeill, William H. *The Shape of European History*. Oxford University Press, 1974.

Miller, Barnette. *Beyond the Sublime Porte: The Grand Seraglio of Stambul*. Yale University Press, 1931.

———. *The Palace School of Muhammed the Conquerer*. Harvard University Press, 1941.

Miller, James. *The Passion of Michel Foucault*. Simon and Schuster, 1993.

Moon, Parker. *Imperialism and World Politics*. Macmillan, 1926.

Muravchik, Joshua. *The Next Founders: Voices of Democracy in the Middle East*. Encounter, 2009.

Nagel, Thomas. *Secular Philosophy and the Religious Temperament*. Oxford University Press, 2010.

Nasr, Vali. *Forces of Fortune: The Rise of the New Muslim Middle Class and What it Will Mean for Our World*. Free Press, 2010.

Newman, John Henry. "The Turks in Their Relation to Europe." In *Historical Sketches*, vol. 1. Longmans, Green, 1901.

Nicholl, Charles. *Somebody Else: Arthur Rimbaud in Africa 1880–91*. University of Chicago Press, 1991.

Nicolle, David. *The Great Islamic Conquests A.D. 632–750*. Osprey, 2009.

Niebuhr, Reinhold and Paul E. Sigmund. *The Democratic Experience: Past and Prospects*. Praeger, 1969.

Pangle, Thomas L. *The Theological Basis of Liberal Modernity in Montesquieu's "Spirit of the Laws."* University of Chicago Press, 2010.

Parry, J. H. *The Age of Reconnaissance*. Mentor, 1964.

Peters, F.E. *The Children of Abraham: Judaism, Christianity, and Islam*. Princeton University Press, 2004.

Pipes, Daniel. *In the Path of God: Islam and Political Power*. Transaction, 2002.

Quinn, Frederick. *The Sum of All Heresies: The Image of Islam in Western Thought*. Oxford University Press, 2008.

Redles, David. *Hitler's Millennial Reich: Apocalyptic Belief and the Search for Salvation*. New York University Press, 2005.

Reischauer, Edwin O. *The Japanese*. Harvard University Press, 1978.

Remini, Robert. *Joseph Smith*. Viking Penguin, 2002.

Riley-Smith, Jonathan. *The Crusades, Christianity, and Islam*. Columbia University Press, 2008.

Royal, Robert. *The God that Did Not Fail*. Encounter, 2006.

Runciman, Steven. *Byzantine Civilization*. Meridian, 1956.

———. *The Fall of Constantinople 1453*. Cambridge University Press, 1969.

Ruthven, Malise. *A Satanic Affair: Salman Rushdie and the Rage of Islam*. Chatto and Windus, 1990.

Schroeder, Paul W. "The Nineteenth Century International System." *World Politics XXXIX*, No. 1, October 1986.

Seton-Watson, R.W. *Disraeli, Gladstone, and the Eastern Question: A Study in Diplomacy and Party Politics*. Norton, 1972.

Setton, Kenneth M. *Western Hostility to Islam and Prophesies of Turkish Doom*. American Philosophic Society, vol. 201, 1992.

Singh, Jyotsna G. *A Companion to the Global Renaissance: English Literature and Culture in the Era of Expansion*. Wiley-Blackwell, 2009.

Sizgorich, Thomas. "'Do Prophets Come With a Sword?' Conquest, Empire, and Historical Narrative in the Early Islamic World." *American Historical Review*, October 2007, 993–1015.

Smith, Lee. *The Strong Horse: Power, Politics, and the Clash of Arab Civilizations*. Doubleday, 2010.

Sonnino, Paul. *Mazarin's Quest: The Congress of Westphalia and the Coming of the Fronde*. Harvard University Press, 2008.

Spencer, Vicki A. "Viewing Islam Through Enlightenment Eyes," in *Western Political Thought in Dialogue with Asia*. Shogimen and Nederman, eds. Lexington Books, 2009.

Sternhell, Zeev. *The Anti-Enlightenment Tradition*. Yale University Press, 2010.

Strachan, Hew. *The First World War*. Viking, 2003.

Suri, Jeremi. *Henry Kissinger and the American Century*. Harvard University Press, 2007.

Taheri, Amir. "The Crackup of the Arab Tyrannies?" *The Weekly Standard*. July 7/14, 2003. pp. 28–31.

Tanner, Marie. *The Last Descendant of Aeneas: The Hapsburgs and the Mythic Image of the Emperor*. Yale University Press, 1993.

Taylor, William R. *Cavalier and Yankee: The Old South and American National Character*. Harvard University Press, 1979.

Thorne, Christopher. *The Issue of War: States, Societies, and the Far Eastern Conflict of 1941–1945*. Oxford University Press, 1985.

Tidrick, Kathryn. *Heart-Beguiling Araby*. Cambridge University Press, 1981.

Till, Nicholas. *Mozart and the Enlightenment: Truth, Virtue and Beauty in Mozart's Operas*. Norton, 1992.

Toynbee, Arnold. "The Collapse of the Caliphate." *Annual Survey of International Affairs*. British Institute of International Affairs, vol. 1924.

Trevor-Roper, Hugh. *History and the Enlightenment*. Yale University Press, 2010.

Trofimov, Yaroslav. *The Siege of Mecca: The Forgotten Uprising in Islam's Holiest Shrine and the Birth of al-Qaeda*. Doubleday, 2007.

Valensi, Lucette. *The Birth of the Despot: Venice and the Sublime Porte*. Trans. Arthur Denner. Cornell University Press, 1993.

Watt, W. Montgomery. *Muslim Intellectual: A Study of Al-Ghazali*. Edinburgh: The University Press, 1963.

Wawro, Geoffrey. *The Franco-Prussian War: The German Conquest of France in 1870–1871*. Cambridge University Press, 2003.

Weigel, George. *Faith, Reason, and the War Against Jihadism*. Doubleday, 2007.

Willmott, H.P. *Empires in the Balance: Japanese and Allied Pacific Strategies to April 1942*. Naval Institute Press, 1982.

Zumwalt, Elmo R., Jr. *On Watch: A Memoir*. Quadrangle, 1976.

About the Author

CHARLES HILL, a career minister in the U.S. Foreign Service, is a research fellow at the Hoover Institution and cochair of the Working Group on Islamism and the International Order. He was executive aide to former U.S. secretary of state George P. Shultz (1983–89) and served as special consultant on policy to the secretary-general of the United Nations from 1992 to 1996. He is also Brady-Johnson Distinguished Fellow in Grand Strategy at Yale University, where he is Senior Lecturer in the Humanities.

Among Hill's awards are the Superior Honor Award from the Department of State in 1973 and 1981; the Distinguished Honor Award in 1978; the Presidential Meritorious Service Award in 1986; the Presidential Distinguished Service Award in 1987; and the Secretary of State's Medal in 1989. He was granted an honorary doctor of laws degree by Rowan University.

Hill received an A.B. degree from Brown University and an M.A. and J.D. from the University of Pennsylvania. He was awarded an LL.D. (Hon.) from Rowan University.

Hill has collaborated with former U.N. Secretary General Boutros Boutros-Ghali on *Egypt's Road to Jerusalem*, a memoir of the Middle East peace negotiations, and *Unvanquished*, about U.S. relations with the U.N. in the post–cold war period, both published by Random House. Hill is the editor of the three-volume *Papers of U.N. Secretary-General Boutros-Ghali*, published by Yale University Press. His *Grand Strategies: Literature, Statecraft, and World Order* was published by Yale in 2010.

HERBERT AND JANE DWIGHT
WORKING GROUP ON
ISLAMISM AND THE
INTERNATIONAL ORDER

The Herbert and Jane Dwight Working Group on Islamism and the International Order seeks to engage in the task of reversing Islamic radicalism through reforming and strengthening the legitimate role of the state across the entire Muslim world. Efforts will draw on the intellectual resources of an array of scholars and practitioners from within the United States and abroad, to foster the pursuit of modernity, human flourishing, and the rule of law and reason in Islamic lands—developments that are critical to the very order of the international system.

The Working Group is chaired by Hoover fellows Fouad Ajami and Charles Hill with an active participation of Director John Raisian. Current core membership includes Russell A. Berman, Abbas Milani, and Shelby Steele, with contributions from Zeyno Baran, Reuel Marc Gerecht, Ziad Haider, John Hughes, Nibras Kazimi, Bernard Lewis, Habib Malik, Camille Pecastaing, and Joshua Teitelbaum.

INDEX